MICROSOFT WORKS
in easy steps

Stephen Copestake

In easy steps is an imprint of Computer Step
5c Southfield Road, Southam
Warwickshire CV33 OJH England
☎01926 817999

First published 1996
Copyright © 1996 by Computer Step

For all sales and volume discounts please contact Computer Step on
Tel: 01926 817999.

For translation rights and export orders write to the address above or
Fax: (+44) 1926 817005.

Printed and bound in England

ISBN 1-874029-41-5

HANDY REFERENCE - Keyboard shortcuts

Works as a whole

Ctrl+N .... Launches the Task Launcher
Ctrl+O ....Opens an existing file
Ctrl+S .... Saves the active document
Ctrl+P .... Prints the active document
Ctrl+G (or F5) .... Launches the Go To dialog
Ctrl+W .... Closes the active document
Ctrl+B .... Emboldens (or removes emboldening)
Ctrl+I .... Italicises (or removes italicisation)
Ctrl+U .... Underlines (or removes underlining)
Ctrl+F .... Launches a find operation
Ctrl+H ....Launches a search-and-replace operation
Ctrl+A .... Select All command
Ctrl+Z .... Undo/Reverse Undo

Word Processor-specific

Ctrl+Shift+F .... Activates the Font Name button in the toolbar
Ctrl+Shift+P .... Activates the Font Size button in the Formatting toolbar
Ctrl+E ....Centres text
Ctrl+L .... Left-justifies text
Ctrl+J .... Applies full (right and left) justification to text
Ctrl+M ....Applies an indent
F7 .... Launches a spell check
Shift+F7 .... Launches the Thesaurus

Spreadsheet-specific

F8 .... Toggles Selection mode on and off
Ctrl+Shift+F8 .... Alternative Select All command
F2 .... Launches Edit Mode
Ctrl+R .... Fill Right
Ctrl+D .... Fill Down
Ctrl+; .... Inserts the current date
Ctrl+Shift+: .... Inserts the current time
F7 .... Launches a spell check

Database-specific

F9 .... Switches to Form view
Shift+F9 .... Switches to List view
Ctrl+F9 .... Switches to Form Design view
Ctrl+R .... Fill Right
Ctrl+D .... Fill Down
Ctrl+; .... Inserts the current date
Ctrl+Shift+: .... Inserts the current time
F7 .... Launches a spell check
Ctrl+Shift+F8 .... Alternative Select All command (only in List view)

ABOUT THE SERIES

In easy steps series is developed for time-sensitive people who want results fast. It is designed for quick, easy and effortless learning.

By using the best authors in the field, and with our experience in writing computer training materials, this series is ideal for today's computer users. It explains the essentials simply, concisely and clearly - without the unnecessary verbal blurb. We strive to ensure that each book is technically superior, effective for easy learning and offers the best value.

Learn the essentials **in easy steps** - accept no substitutes!

Titles in the series include:

Title	Author	ISBN
Windows 95	Harshad Kotecha	1-874029-28-8
Microsoft Office	Stephen Copestake	1-874029-37-7
Internet UK	Andy Holyer	1-874029-31-8
CompuServe UK	John Clare	1-874029-33-4
CorelDRAW	Stephen Copestake	1-874029-32-6
PageMaker	Scott Basham	1-874029-35-0
Quicken UK	John Sumner	1-874029-30-X
Microsoft Works	Stephen Copestake	1-874029-41-5
Word	Scott Basham	1-874029-39-3
Excel	Pamela Roach	1-874029-40-7
Sage	Ralf Kirchmayr	1-874029-43-1
SmartSuite	Stephen Copestake	1-874029-42-3

To order or for details on forthcoming titles ask your bookseller or contact Computer Step on 01926 817999.

Contents

4. The Database 121

A Common Approach

This chapter shows you how Works provides a common look, so you can get started quickly in any module. You'll learn how to create new documents and open/save existing ones. You'll also learn how to get information you need from Works' on-line HELP system, and how to use Note-It, the inbuilt Works notation utility.

Covers

Introduction (1)

Microsoft Works consists of three principal modules:

- The Word Processor

- The Spreadsheet

- The Database

In a sense, these are 'cut-down' versions of Microsoft Word, Excel and Access. In spite of this, however, all three modules provide a high level of functionality and ease of use.

Another advantage of Works is that it integrates the three modules exceptionally well. The modules share a common look and feel.

The illustration below shows the Word Processor opening screen. Flagged are components which are common to the other modules, too.

Works also provides a further module: Communications. However, this isn't covered within this book. Any reference to 'Works modules' therefore refers solely to the Word Processor, Spreadsheet & Database.

Although the toolbar appears in each Works module, the contents vary somewhat from module to module.

For how to use and customise the toolbar, see later in this section.

Introduction (2)

Compare this with the following:

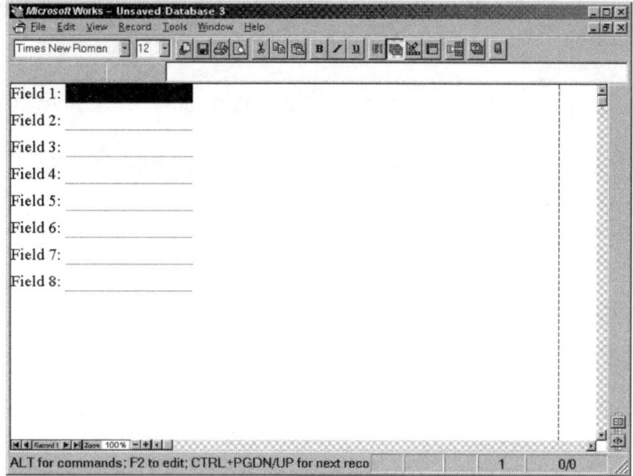

Database screen

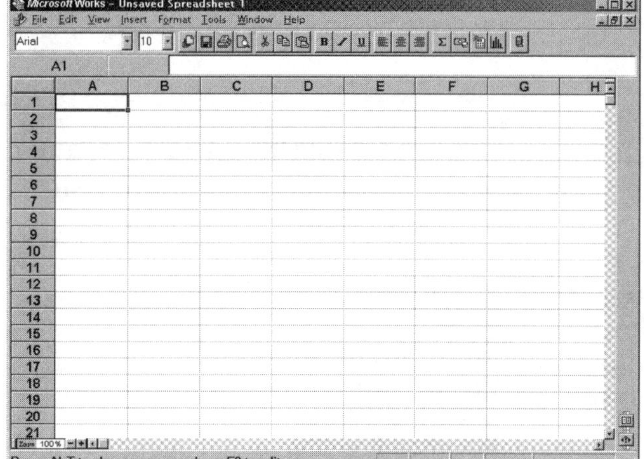

Spreadsheet screen

There are, of course, differences between the module screens; we'll explore these in later sections.

Notice that many of the screen components are held in common. The purpose of this shared approach is to ensure that users of Works can move between modules with the minimum of readjustment.

The Works toolbar (1)

The toolbar is an important component in all three Works modules. A toolbar is an on-screen bar which contains shortcut buttons. These symbolise and allow easy access to often used commands which would normally have to be invoked via one or more menus.

For example, The Word Processor's toolbar lets you:

*   launch other modules

*   create, open, save and print documents

*   perform copy-and-paste and cut-and-paste operations

*   align text

*   embolden, italicise or underline text

*   apply a new typeface and/or type size to text

*   spell-check text

by simply clicking on the relevant button.

The toolbar varies to some extent from module to module.

Hiding/revealing the toolbar

In the Word Processor, Spreadsheet or Database, pull down the View menu. Do the following:

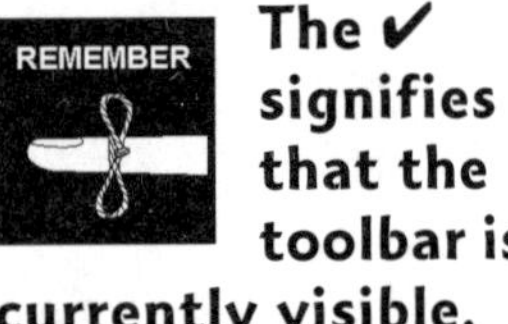

The ✔ signifies that the toolbar is currently visible.

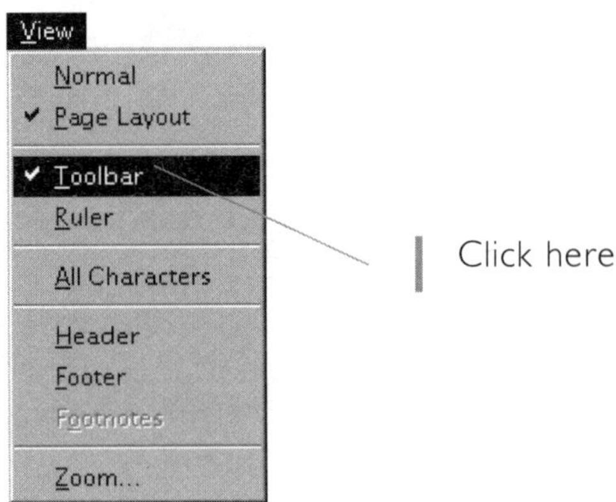

Click here

The Works toolbar (2)

Adding buttons to the toolbar

By default, the pre-defined toolbar which appears in the
Works modules has only a small number of buttons
associated with it. For instance, the Word Processor version
has 18. However, just about all editing operations you can
perform from within Works menus can be incorporated as
a button within the toolbar, for ease of access.

To do this, first make sure the toolbar is visible on-screen
(see earlier for how to do this). Pull down the Tools menu
and click Customize Toolbar. Now do the following:

Click the menu to which you want
the button added

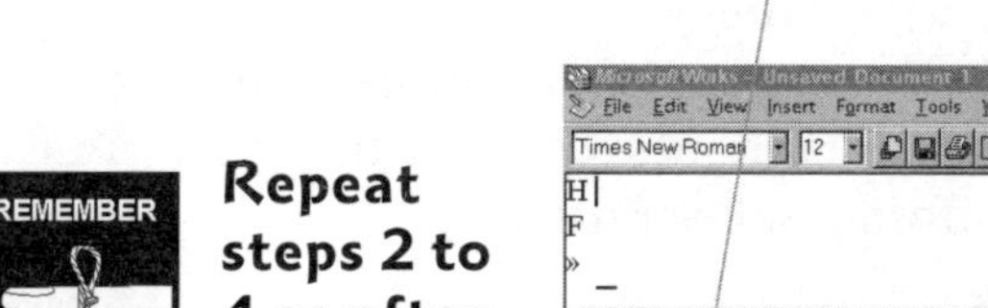

3 Drag it onto the toolbar

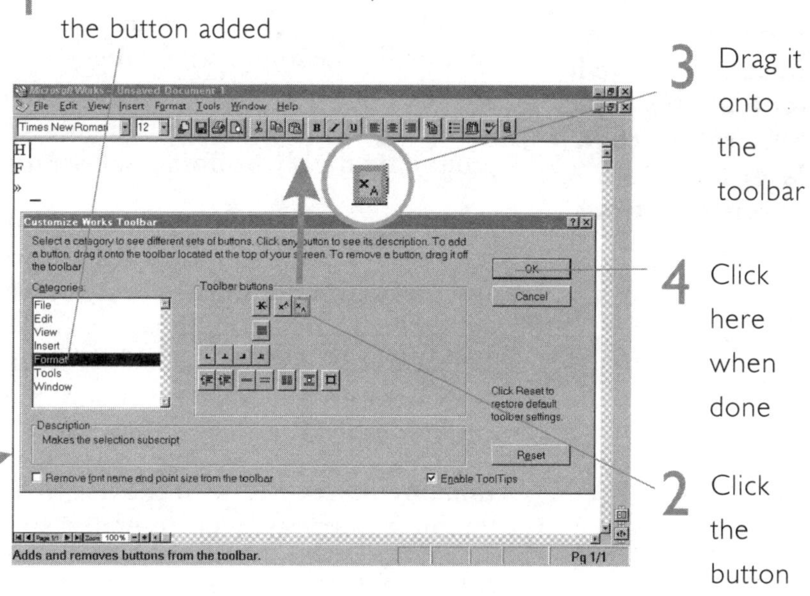

4 Click here when done

Click Reset to restore default toolbar settings.

2 Click the button

REMEMBER

Repeat steps 2 to 4 as often as necessary.

HANDY TIP

If in doubt, left-click any button in the dialog and hold down the mouse button; Works tells you what it does in the Description field.

Removing buttons from the toolbar

If you no longer want a button to appear on the toolbar,
pull down the Tools menu and click Customize Toolbar.
When the Customize Works Toolbar dialog has launched
(see above), click the relevant button. Drag it off the
toolbar. Then follow step 4 above.

New document creation

All Works modules let you:

- create new blank documents

- create new documents with the help of a 'TaskWizard'

- create new documents based on a 'template' you've created yourself

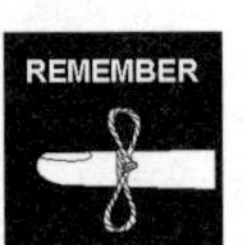

Because the Word Processor, Database and Spreadsheet modules are uniform in the way they create new documents, we'll look at this topic here rather than in later module-specific sections.

Creating blank documents is the simplest route to new document creation; use this if you want to define the document components yourself from scratch. This is often not the most efficient way to create new documents.

TaskWizards are a shortcut to the creation of new documents. You work through a series of dialogs, answering the appropriate questions and making the relevant choices. TaskWizards greatly simplify and speed up the creation of new documents while at the same time producing highly professional results.

Templates are sample documents complete with the relevant formatting and/or text. Works doesn't come with any pre-written templates, but you can save your own documents (including those created with the help of TaskWizards) as templates for future use. By basing a new document on a template, you automatically have access to any inherent text and/or formatting.

Documents created with the use of TaskWizards or templates can easily be amended subsequently.

All three document creation methods involve launching the Works Task Launcher. This is a useful composite dialog which you can also use to open existing Works documents.

For more information on opening Works documents, see later.

Creating blank documents

You can create a new blank document from within any of the Works modules.

The first step is to launch the Task Launcher. From within the relevant module, pull down the File menu and click New. Now do the following:

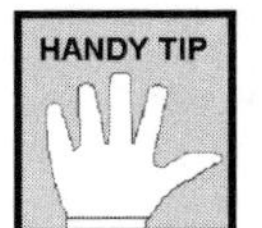

You can use a keyboard shortcut to run the Task Launcher. Simply press Ctrl+N.

Ensure this tab is active

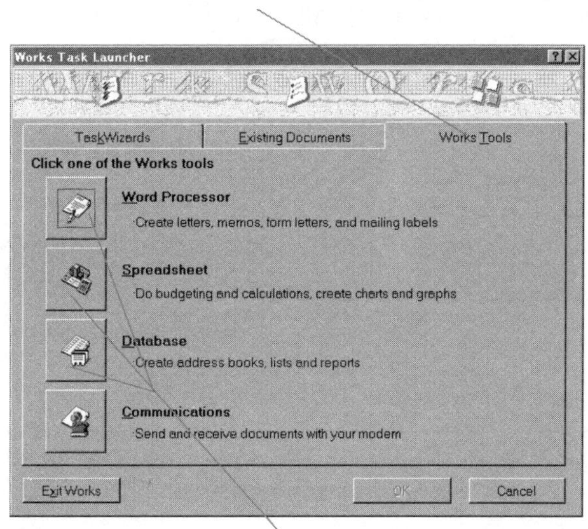

2 Click the relevant module

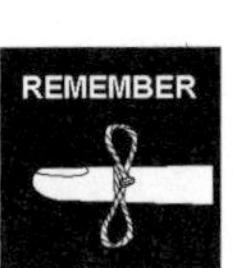

If you're creating a new database, Works doesn't immediately comply; before it can do so, you need to define the necessary fields. See Section 4 for how to do this.

Running Task Launcher automatically

If you want to create a new blank document immediately after you've started Works, you don't need to launch the Task Launcher manually: it appears automatically.

Once the Task Launcher is on-screen, however, you can follow the above steps to produce the relevant blank document.

Using TaskWizards (1)

Works provides a large number of TaskWizards, organised under overall category headings. With these, you can create a very wide variety of professional-quality documents. For example, you can create newsletters, CVs, letterheads, memos, brochures, bids, labels, quotations, fax sheets, employee profiles, invoices, phone lists, certificates, theses, school reports, tests...

Basing new documents on a TaskWizard

In any of the three principal Works modules, pull down the File menu and click New. The Task Launcher appears. Carry out the following steps:

Ensure this tab is active

The section on the right of the Task Launcher provides a potted description of the selected TaskWizard.

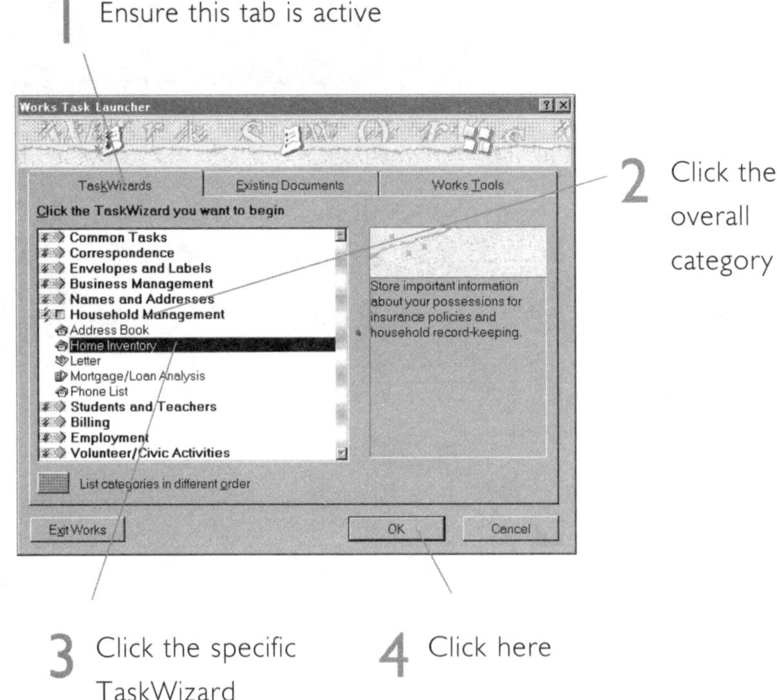

2 Click the overall category

3 Click the specific TaskWizard

4 Click here

Works now launches a series of question-and-answer dialogs.

Using TaskWizards (2)

When you've selected the TaskWizard you want to use, Works launches a series of dialogs which vary accordingly. However, the basic format is the same. Works is asking you to supply it with the minimal information required.

The illustration below is the first stage in most or all TaskWizards. Perform the action indicated.

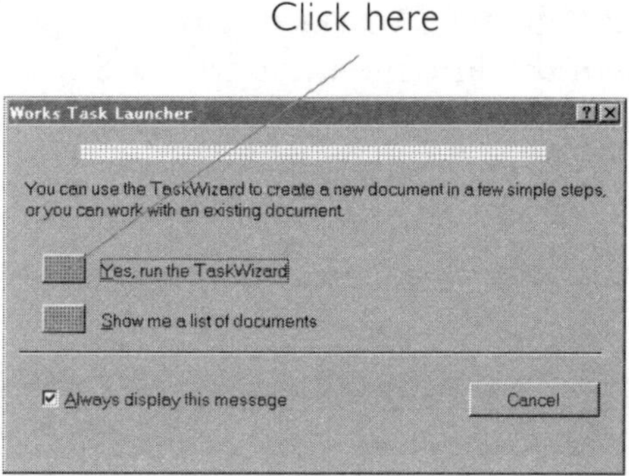

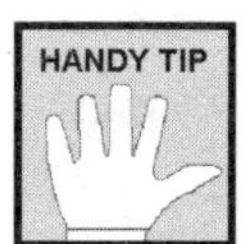

Works tells you when you've reached the final dialog by dimming the Next button.

Complete the next dialog as appropriate. To move on to the next dialog when you've finished, click the Next button. Do this as often as necessary until you reach the final TaskWizard dialog. Then do the following:

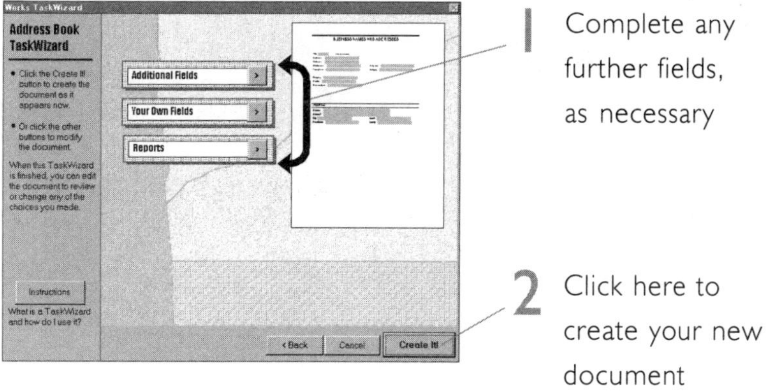

Using templates

In any Works module, you can save an existing document (complete with all text and formatting) as a template. You can then use the template as the basis for new document creation. The text/formatting is immediately carried across.

Saving your work as a template

First, open the document you want to save as a template (for how to do this, see the 'Opening Works documents (1)' and 'Opening Works documents (2)' topics later). Pull down the File menu and click Save As. Now do the following:

1 Click here. In the drop-down list, click the drive you want to host the template

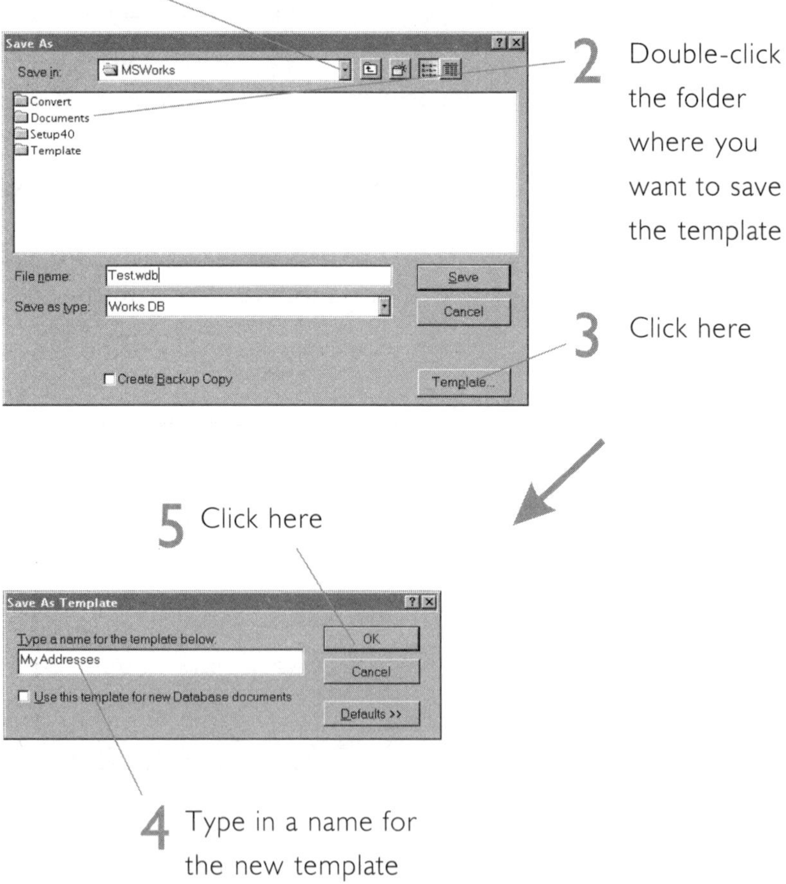

2 Double-click the folder where you want to save the template

3 Click here

5 Click here

4 Type in a name for the new template

Opening Works documents (1)

We saw earlier that Works lets you create new documents in various ways. You can also open Word Processor, Spreadsheet and Database documents you've already created:

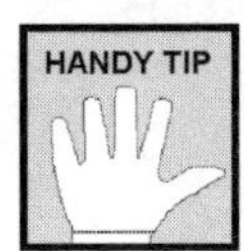

You can also use the Documents section of the Windows 95 Startup menu to open recently used Works files - see your Windows 95 documentation for how to do this.

- just after you've started Works

- from within the relevant Works module

Opening an existing document at startup

Immediately after you've started Works, carry out steps 1 and 2, or 1 and 3, as appropriate:

Ensure this tab is active

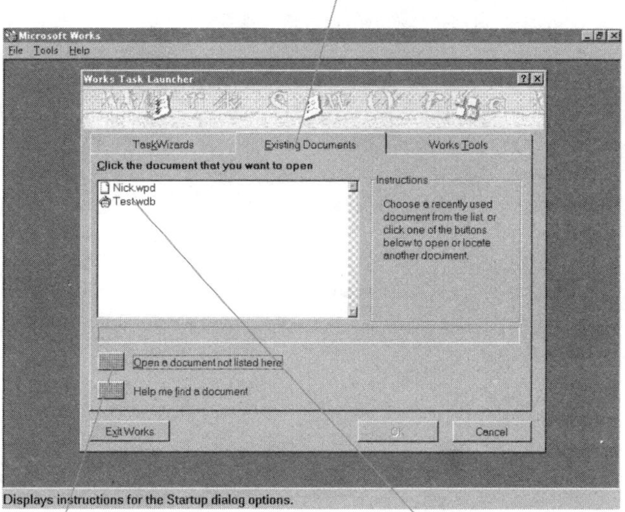

3 Click here if the existing file you need isn't shown in step 2

2 Double-click a recently used file to open it

If you follow steps 1 and 3, the Open dialog appears. See page 18 for how to complete this.

Opening Works documents (2)

You can use a keyboard shortcut to launch the Open dialog: simply press Ctrl+O.

Opening a document from within a module

From within any Works module, pull down the File menu and click Open. Now carry out the following steps, as appropriate:

2 Click here. In the drop-down list, click the drive which hosts the file

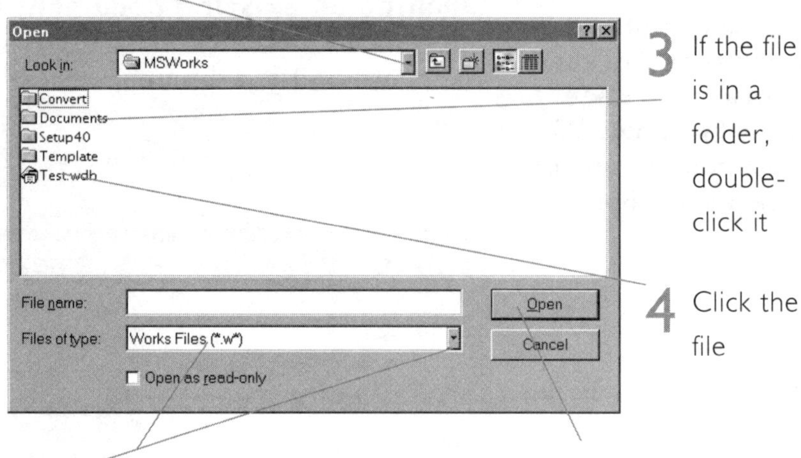

3 If the file is in a folder, double-click it

4 Click the file

| Make sure Works Files is shown. If it isn't, click the arrow and select it from the drop-down list

5 Click here

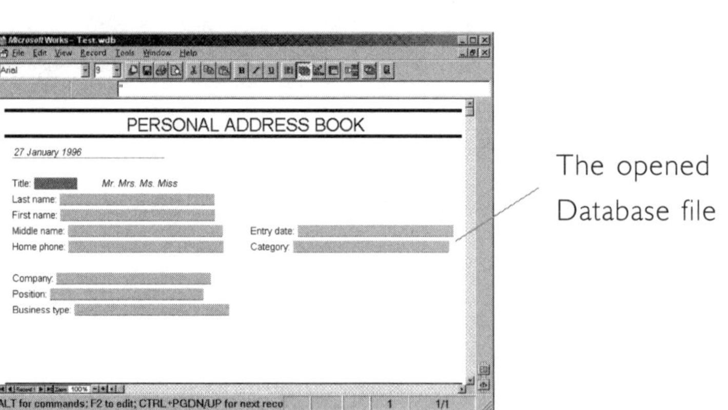

The opened Database file

Saving Works documents

It's important to save your work at frequent intervals, in order to avoid data loss in the event of a hardware fault or power interruption. Works uses a consistent approach to saving.

Saving a document for the first time

In the Word Processor, Spreadsheet or Database modules, pull down the File menu and click Save. Or press Ctrl+S. Now do the following:

2 Click here. In the drop-down list, click the drive you want to host the document

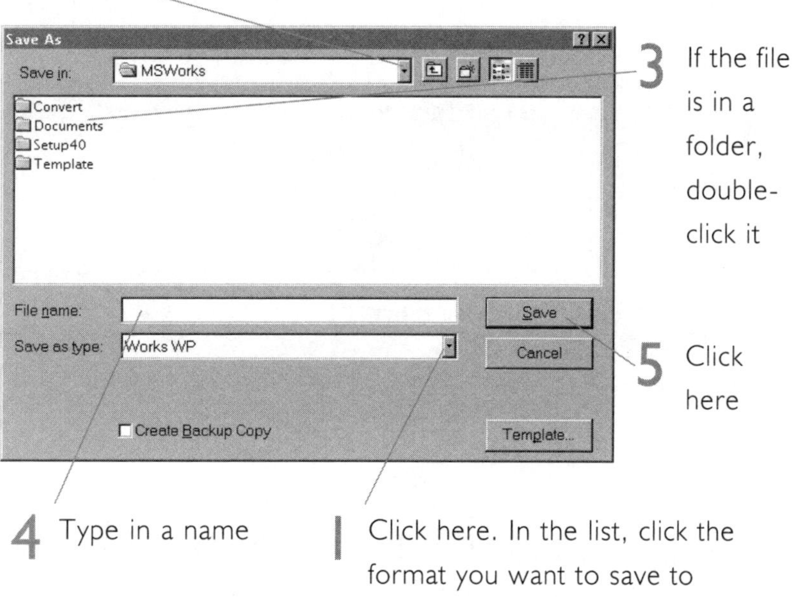

3 If the file is in a folder, double-click it

5 Click here

4 Type in a name

1 Click here. In the list, click the format you want to save to

Saving previously saved documents

In any of the principal modules, pull down the File menu and click Save. Or press Ctrl+S. No dialog launches; instead, Works saves the latest version of your document to disk, overwriting the previous version.

Using Note-It (1)

Note-It lets you insert notes in Word Processor, Spreadsheet or Database documents. Notes consist of text, together with a picture which serves as a marker. The picture is also used to display the associated text. Additionally, notes can have explanatory captions.

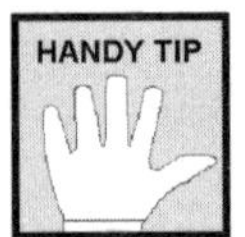

To add a note to a database, you must be in Form Design View (see Section 4 for more information).

Creating a note

Open the document to which you want to add the note. Position the insertion point at the location where you want the note to appear. Pull down the Insert menu and click Note-It. Now do the following:

Click the picture you want to use

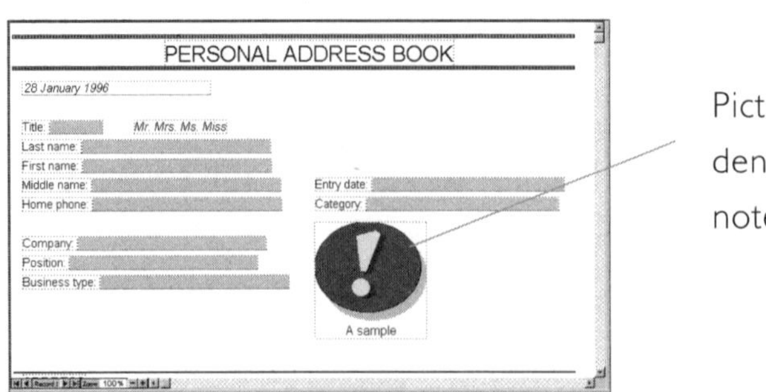

4 Click here to insert the note

2 Type in caption text

3 Type your note

The illustration below shows a database with an inserted note:

Note - pictures can be moved and resized in the normal way.

Picture marker denoting inserted note

Using Note-It (2)

Viewing inserted notes

First, click the note to select it. Then pull down the Edit menu and do the following:

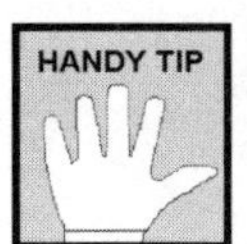

Another way to view an inserted note is simply to double-click on it.

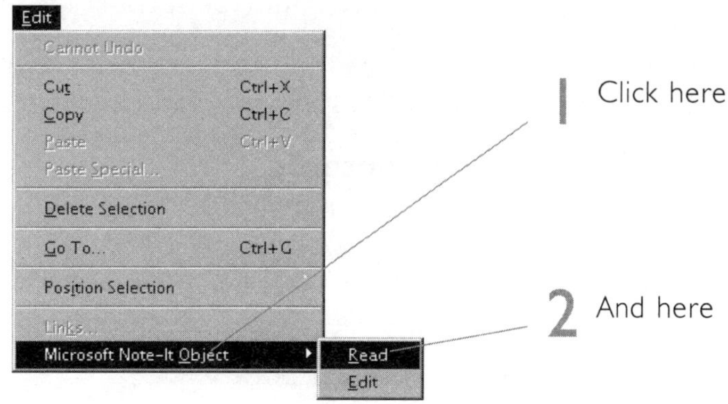

Click here

1

And here

2

The next illustration shows a note displayed over a database:

Magnified view of note

To amend an existing note, click on it. Pull down the Edit menu and click Microsoft Note-It Object. Click Edit in the sub-menu. For how to complete the Microsoft Note-It dialog, see the 'Using Note-It (1)' topic.

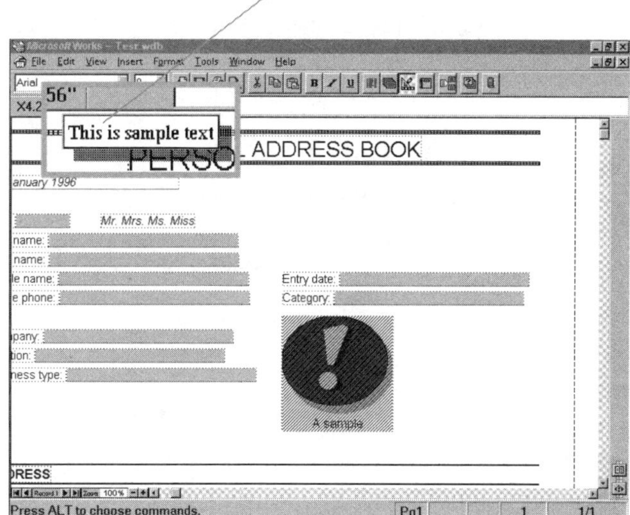

Using the Works HELP system (1)

Works has comprehensive HELP facilities, organised under two broad headings:

- Contents (a list of topics organised by module)

- Index (an alphabetical list of topics)

To generate either of these from within any module, pull down the HELP menu and choose Contents or Index.

Using Contents

Do the following:

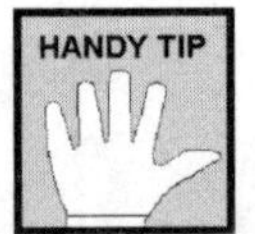
You can use a keyboard shortcut to launch Help: simply press F1. Then click on the Index or Contents tabs, as appropriate, and follow the relevant steps.

Click the relevant module

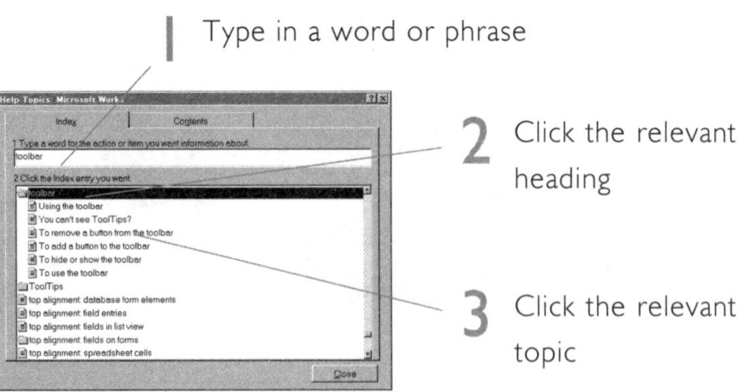

2 Click the relevant heading

3 Click here to close Contents

After step 2, Works launches a series of sub-headings. When you find the topic you want information on (prefixed by 🗎 instead of 🗀), click on it.

Using Index

Do the following:

Type in a word or phrase

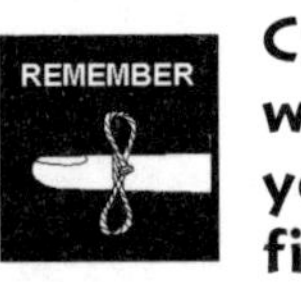
Click Close when you've finished using Index.

2 Click the relevant heading

3 Click the relevant topic

Using the Works HELP system (2)

When you've used the Contents or Index sections of HELP to pick the topic you want help with, Works displays it as a separate window by the side of the open document. Carry out steps 1-4 below, as appropriate:

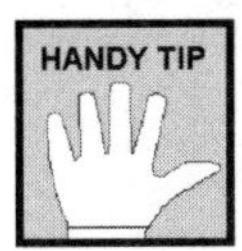

Re step 2 - to view one of the related topics, move the mouse pointer over it and left-click once.

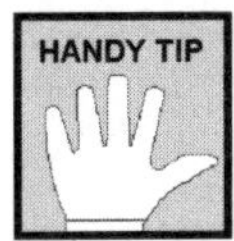

When you carry out step 3, the open document expands to fill the document window.

HELP topic

Click here for a list of related topics

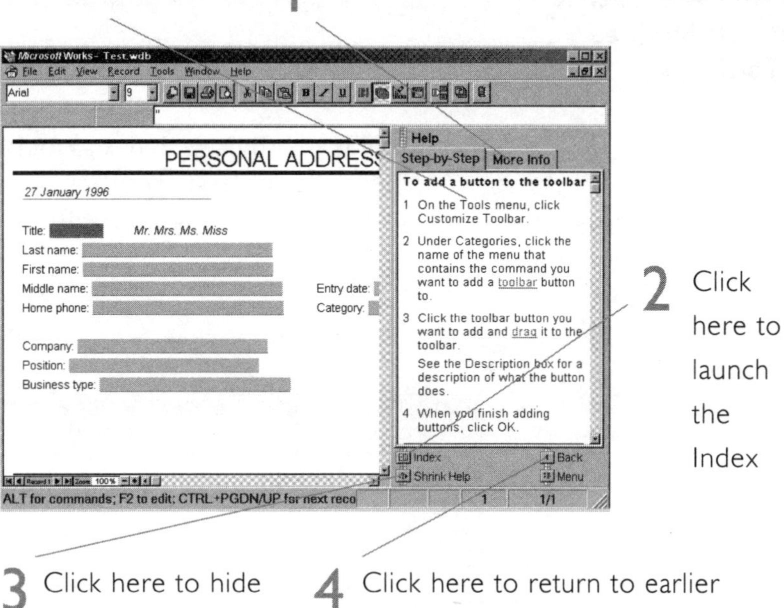

2 Click here to launch the Index

3 Click here to hide the HELP topic

4 Click here to return to earlier topic (if applicable)

Sometimes, selecting a topic in the Index or Contents sections of the HELP system produces a different result:

Click on any link (denoted by underlining) to display a special HELP box providing further information.

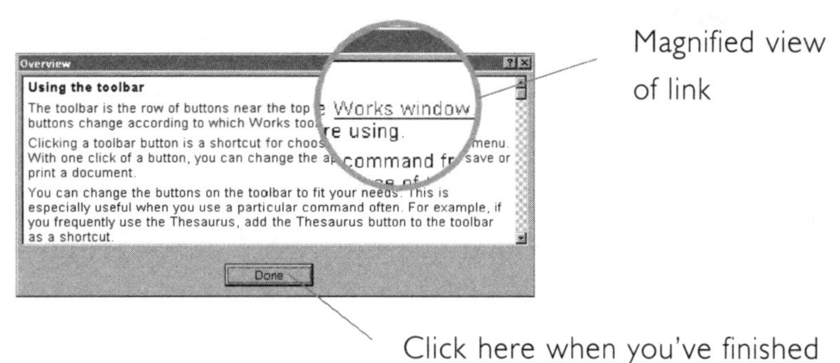

Magnified view of link

Click here when you've finished

Using the Works HELP system (3)

There are more immediate ways to get help:

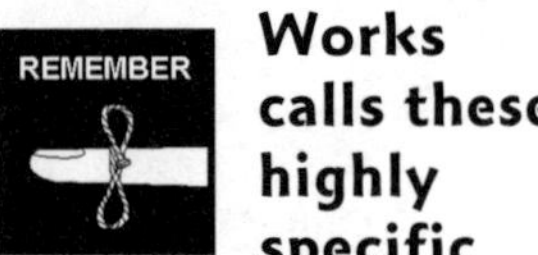

Works calls these highly specific HELP bubbles 'ToolTips'.

- Moving the mouse pointer over toolbar buttons produces an explanatory HELP bubble:

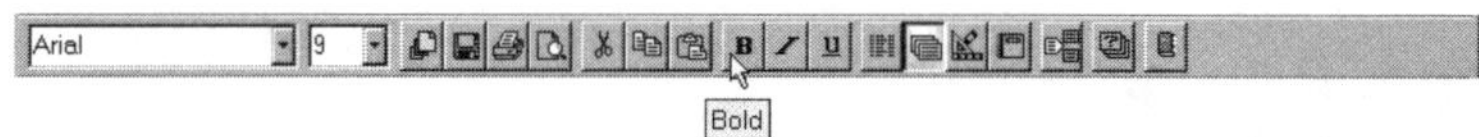

- Fields in dialogs have associated HELP boxes. To view a box, first, right-click in a field. Then carry out the following procedure:

Left-click here for the specific HELP topic

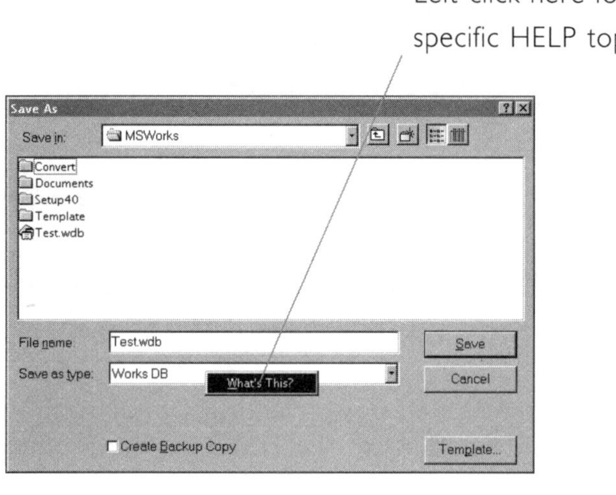

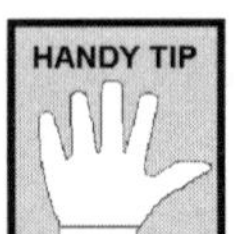

When you've finished with a HELP box, press Esc to close it.

Other standard Windows 95 HELP features are also present; see your Windows documentation for how to use these.

The Word Processor

This chapter gives you the basics of using the Word Processor. You'll learn how to enter text and negotiate the screen. You'll also discover how to format text/apply Easy Formats. Finally, you'll learn to insert pictures using the ClipArt Gallery, and then customise page layout/printing.

Covers

The Word Processor screen

Below is an illustration of the Word Processor screen.

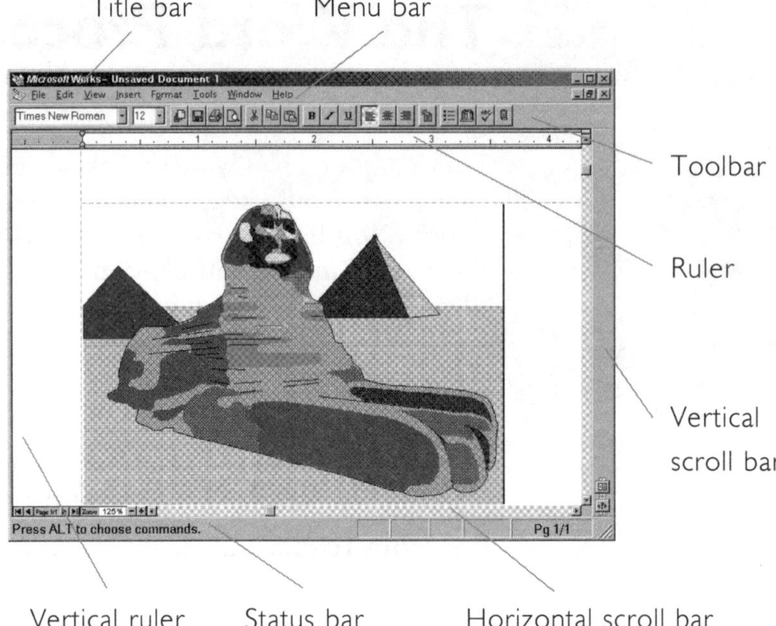

The Status bar displays information relating to the active document (e.g. what page you're on, and the total number of pages).

Some of these – e.g. the ruler and scroll bars – are standard to just about all programs which run under Windows 95. A few of them can be hidden, if required.

Specifying which screen components display

Pull down the View menu. Then do either of the following:

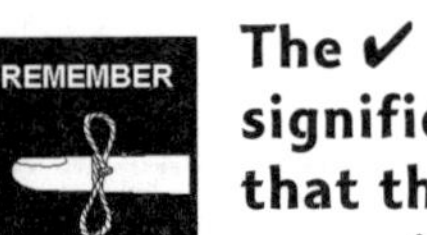

The ✔ signifies that the menu item is currently visible.

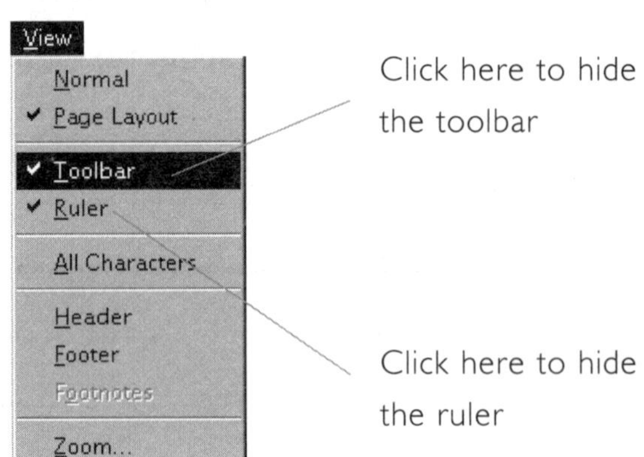

Entering text

The Word Processor lets you enter text immediately after you've started it. You enter text at the insertion point:

A magnified view of the text insertion point

Begin entering text here

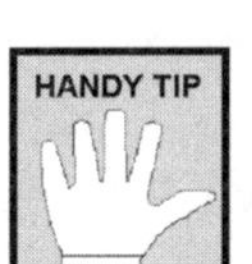 **The Word Processor has automatic word wrap. This means that you don't have to press Return to enter text on a new line; a new line is automatically started for you, when required. Only press Return if you need to begin a new paragraph.**

Overtyping selected text

By default, if you select text and then begin typing, the Word Processor replaces this with the new text automatically. This is often a useful way to work with documents. However, you can turn off this feature if you want. When you do this, new text is positioned *in front of* the specified text.

Pull down the Tools menu and click Options. Now do the following:

Ensure this tab is active

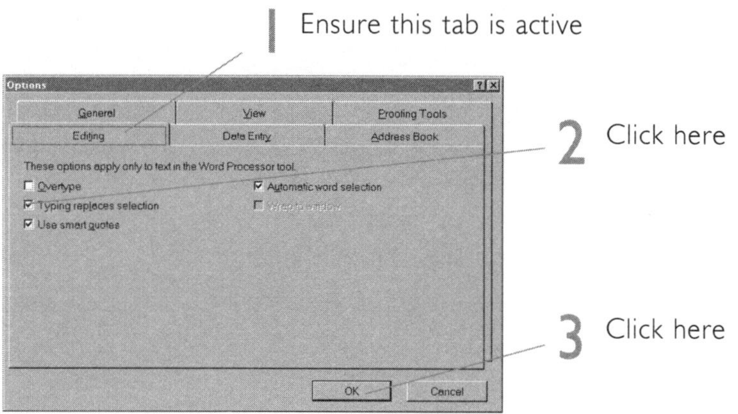

2 Click here

3 Click here

Moving around in documents (1)

You can use the following to move through Word Processor documents:

- keystrokes

- the vertical/horizontal scroll bars

- the Go To dialog

Using keystrokes

Works implements the standard Windows 95 direction keys. Use the left, right, up and down cursor keys in the usual way. Additionally, Home, End, Page Up and Page Down work normally.

Using the scroll bars

Use your mouse to perform any of the following actions;

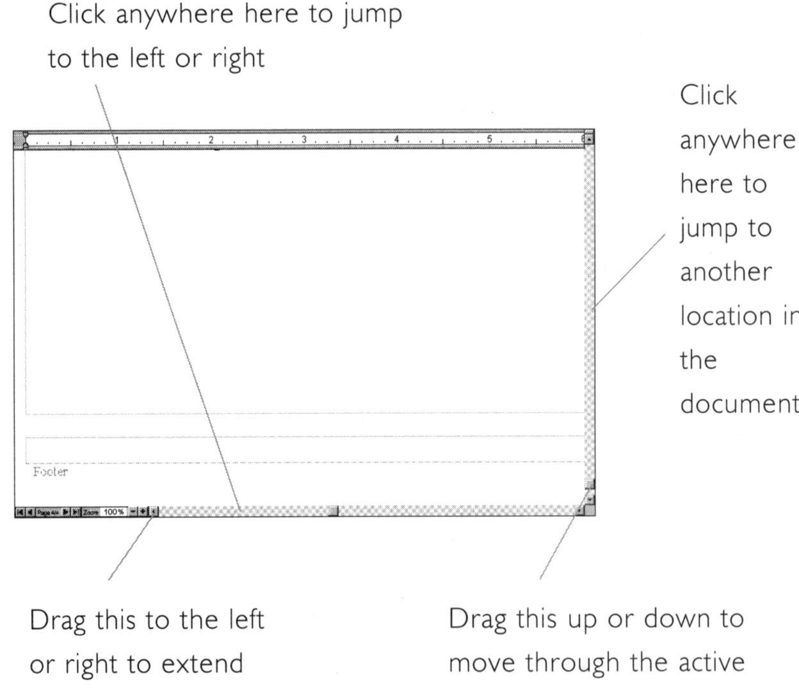

Moving around in documents (2)

Using the Go To dialog

You can use the Go To dialog to move to any page number within the open document.

Pull down the Edit menu and click Go To. Now do the following:

You can use either of two keyboard shortcuts to launch the Go To dialog: simply press Ctrl+G, or F5.

Type in the number of the page you want to jump to

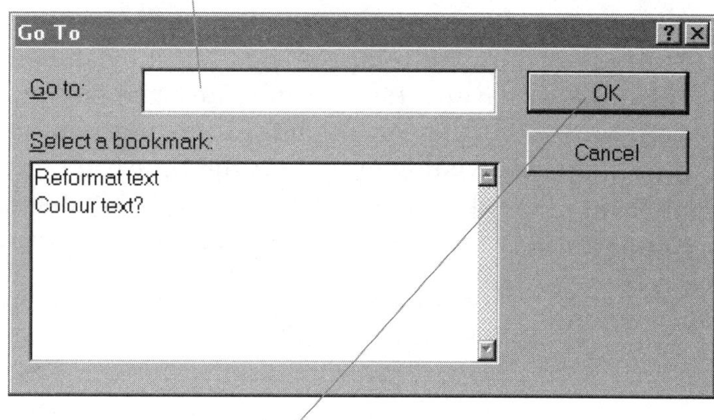

2 Click here

To insert a bookmark into a document, place the insertion point at the relevant location. Pull down the Edit menu and click Bookmark. In the Name field in the Bookmark Name dialog, type in a name. Click OK.

You can also use the Go To dialog to move to a pre-inserted bookmark. Bookmarks are hidden place markers which you can insert into documents at important locations (for instance, in text which you want to revise later, or where you want to add clip art). For how to insert a bookmark, see the tip on the left.

Once you've inserted one or more bookmarks, you can then have the Word Processor jump to the bookmark of your choice.

Launch the Go To dialog, as above. Don't follow step 1 above; instead, in the Select a bookmark field, click the bookmark you want to jump to. Then carry out step 2.

Using views (1)

The Word Processor module lets you examine your work in various ways, according to the approach you need. It calls these 'views'.

There are two principal views:

Normal

Normal View is used for basic text editing. In Normal View, most formatting elements are still visible; for instance, coloured, emboldened or italicised text displays faithfully. Line and page breaks, tabs and paragraph alignments/formatting will display. On the other hand, little attempt is made to show document structure or layout; for example, inserted clip art images invariably display on the left of the page, and headers and footers are invisible except on the first page of the document. Additionally, text will probably display on screen in a way which bears little relation to how it will print.

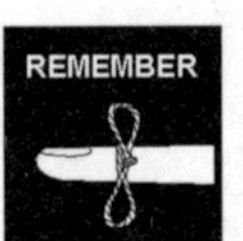

There is a third view which you'll use frequently: Print Preview. See later in this section for more information.

For these reasons, Normal View is quick and easy to use. It's suitable for bulk text entry and editing. It isn't, however, recommended for use with graphics (for this, switch to Page Layout view – see below).

Page Layout

Page Layout – the default – view works like Normal view, with one exception: the positioning of items on the page is reproduced accurately. What you see is a reasonable representation of what your document will look like when printed. Headers and footers are visible, and can be edited directly; margins display faithfully; and pictures occupy their correct position on-screen.

In Page Layout view, the screen is updated more slowly. As a result, use it when your document is nearing completion, for final proofing. This suggestion is particularly apt if you're working with a slow computer.

Using views (2)

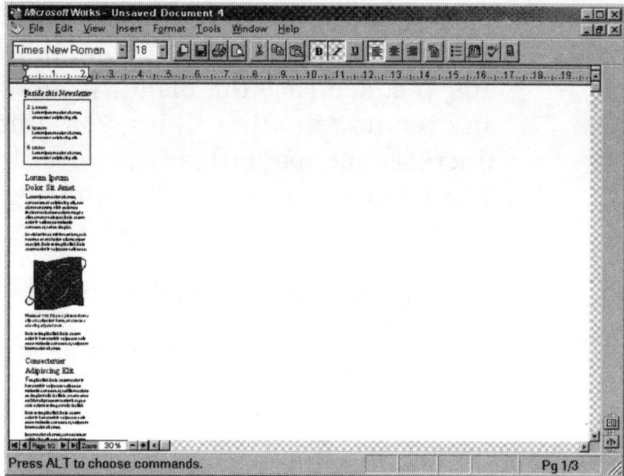

Normal view

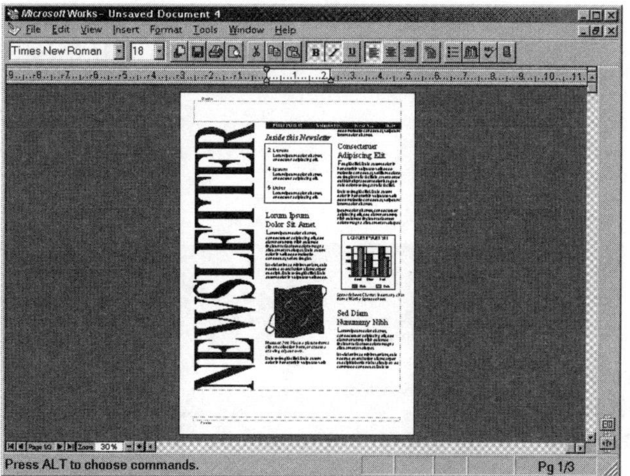

Page Layout view

Switching between Normal & Page Layout views

Pull down the View menu. Click Normal or Page Layout, as appropriate (the view which is currently active has a tick against it).

Changing zoom levels

The ability to vary the level of magnification for the active document is often useful. Sometimes, it's helpful to 'zoom out' (i.e. decrease the magnification) so that you can take an overview; at other times, you'll need to 'zoom in' (increase the magnification) to work in greater detail. The Word Processor module lets you do either of these very easily.

You can do either of the following:

- choose from preset zoom levels (e.g. 100%, 75%)

- specify your own zoom percentage

- choose a zoom setting based on document margins

Setting the zoom level

Pull down the View menu and click Zoom. Now carry out step 1, 2 or 3 below. Then follow step 4.

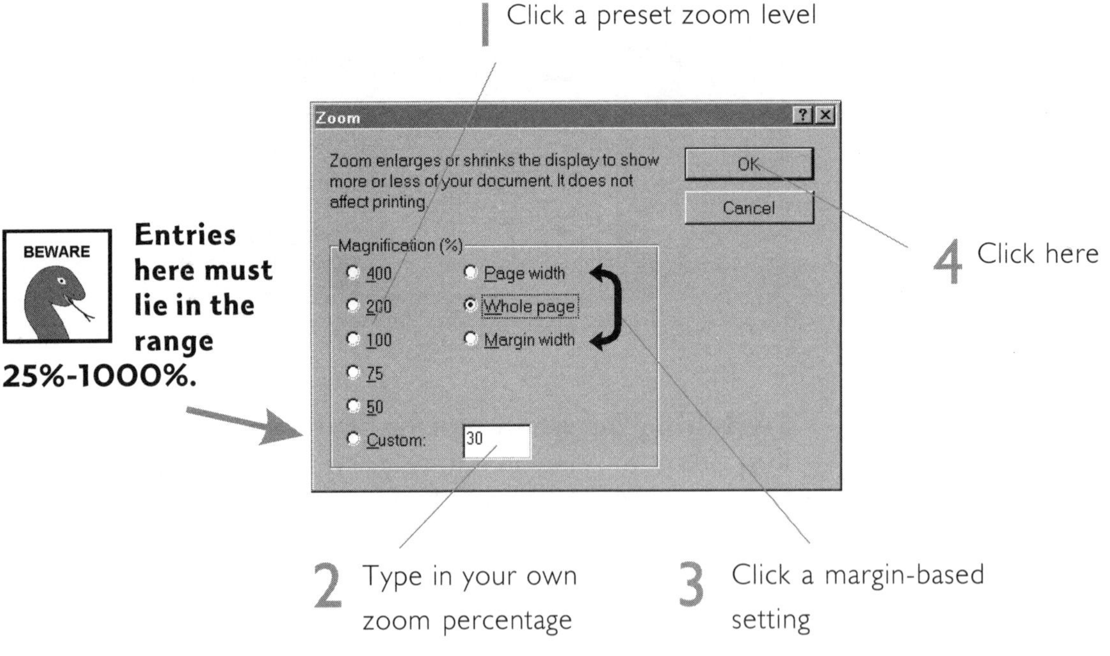

Formatting text - an overview

The Word Processor lets you format text in a variety of ways. Very broadly, however, and for the sake of convenience, text formatting can be divided into two overall categories:

Character formatting

Character formatting is concerned with altering the *appearance* of selected text. Examples include:

- changing the font

- changing the type size

- colouring text

- changing the font style (bold, italic, underlining etc.)

- applying font effects (superscript and subscript)

Character formatting is a misnomer in one sense: it can also be applied to specified paragraphs of text, or to parts of specified paragraphs.

Paragraph formatting

Paragraph formatting has to do with the structuring and layout of paragraphs of text. Examples include:

- specifying paragraph indents

- specifying paragraph alignment (e.g. left or right justification)

- specifying paragraph and line spacing

- imposing borders and/or fills on paragraphs

The Word Processor has a useful text formatting shortcut: Easy Formats. Easy Formats are pre-defined collections of formatting commands which you can apply to selected text in one go.

Changing the font and/or type size

Character formatting can be changed in two ways:

- from within the Font dialog

- (to a lesser extent) by using the toolbar

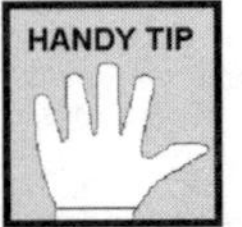

Works uses standard Windows procedures for text selection.

Applying a new font or type size (1)

First, select the text whose typeface and/or type size you want to amend. Pull down the Format menu and click Font and Style. Now carry out steps 1 and/or 2 below. Finally, follow step 3:

Click the font you want to use

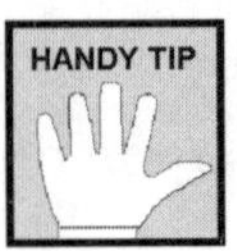

Re step 2 – as well as whole point sizes, you can also enter half-point increments; i.e. the Word Processor will accept 10, 10.5 or 11, but not 10.75.

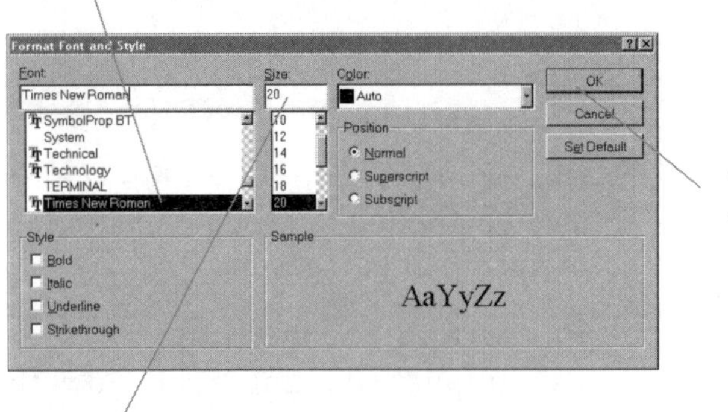

3 Click here

2 Type in the type size you need

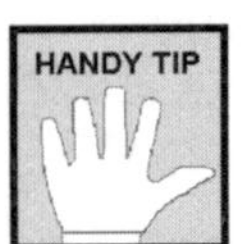

If the toolbar isn't currently visible, pull down the View menu and click Toolbar.

Applying a new font or type size (2)

Make sure the Formatting toolbar is visible. Now select the text you want to amend and do the following:

Click here; select the font you want to use in the drop-down list

Type in the type size you need and press Enter

Changing text colour

You can only change the colour of text by using the Font dialog.

First, select the text you want to alter. Pull down the Format dialog and click Font. Now do the following:

Click here

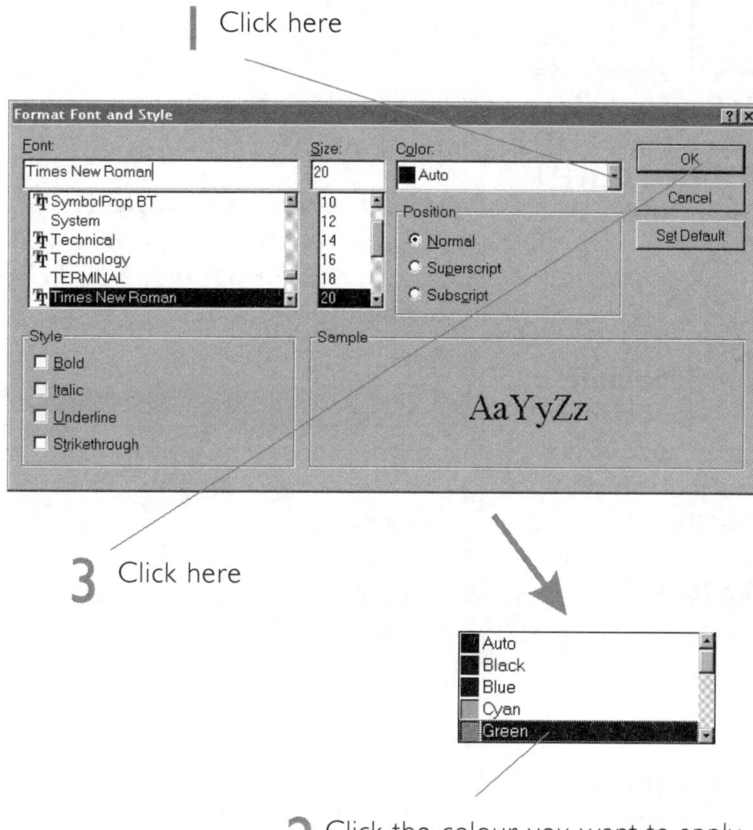

3 Click here

2 Click the colour you want to apply

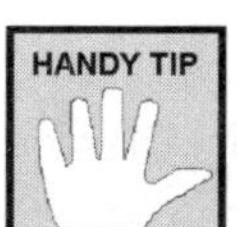

Re step 1 - clicking Auto sets the colour to black (unless you've amended the default Windows text colour).

Removing colours from text

You can use a shortcut to return text to black. First, select the coloured text. Then press Ctrl+Spacebar.

If the text has also had style enhancements (e.g. italicisation) or effects (e.g. superscript) applied to it, these are also removed.

Changing the font style

In the Word Processor, the following styles are available:

- **Bold**
- *Italic*
- <u>Underline</u>
- ~~Strikethrough~~

You can use the Font dialog or the Formatting toolbar to change font styles.

Amending the font style (1)

First, select the text whose style you want to change. Then pull down the Format menu and click Font. Do the following:

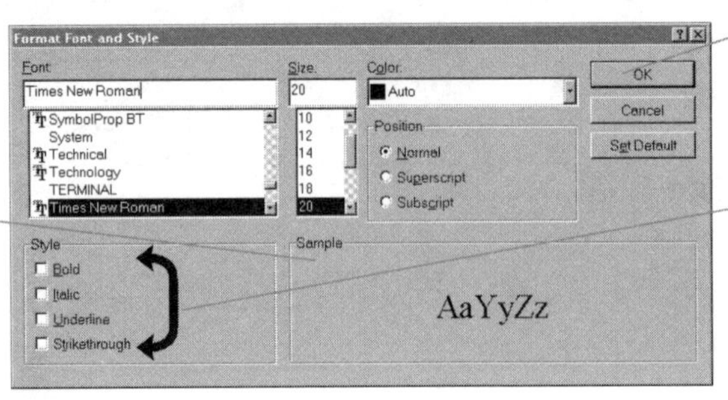

2 Click here

1 Click the font style you want to apply

Amending the font style (2)

First, select the relevant text. Ensure the toolbar is visible. Then do the following:

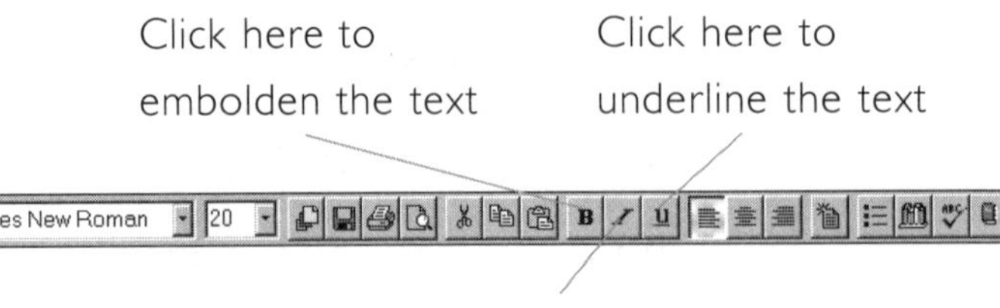

The Sample section provides an indication of what the amendments you make look like.

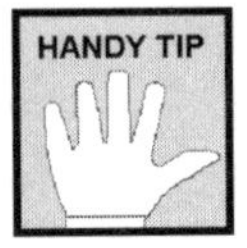

If the toolbar isn't visible, pull down the View menu and click Toolbar.

Font effects

You can use the following font effects in the Word Processor:

- Superscript - e.g. $f^{ont\ effect}$

- Subscript - e.g. $f_{ont\ effect}$

Applying font effects

First, select the relevant text. Pull down the Format dialog and click Font. Then carry out the following steps:

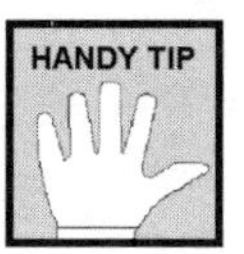

You can also use the following keyboard shortcuts: Ctrl++ for Superscript; Ctrl+= for Subscript.

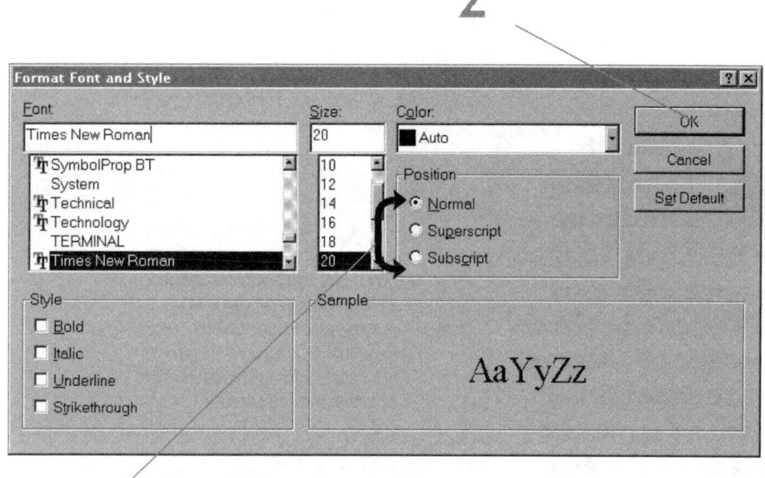

The Superscript and Subscript buttons can be found in the Format category within the Customize Works Toolbar dialog. See the 'The Works toolbar (2)' topic in Section 1.

Using the toolbar to apply effects

As it ships, the Works toolbar *won't* let you superscript or subscript text. However, you can add buttons for these functions easily and quickly.

For how to do this, see the 'The Works toolbar (2)' topic in Section 1.

Indenting paragraphs - an overview

You can achieve a similar effect by using tabs. However, indents are easier to apply (and amend subsequently).

Indents are a crucial component of document layout. For instance, in most document types indenting the first line of paragraphs (i.e. moving it inwards away from the left page margin) makes the text much more legible.

Other document types – e.g. bibliographies – can use the following:

- hanging indents (where the first line is unaltered, while subsequent lines are indented)

- full indents (where the entire paragraph is indented away from the left and/or the right margins)

Some of the potential indent combinations are shown in the illustration below:

Don't confuse indents with page margins. Margins are the gap between the edge of the page and the text area; indents define the distance between the margins and text.

This paragraph has a full left and right indent. It's best, however, not to overdo the extent of the indent: 0.35 inches is often more than adequate.

This paragraph has a first-line indent. This type of indent is suitable for most document types. It's best, however, not to overdo the extent of the indent: 0.35 inches is often more than adequate.

This paragraph has a hanging indent. It's best, however, not to overdo the extent of the indent: 0.35 inches is often more than adequate.

Left and right ('full') indent

First-line indent

Hanging indent

Left margin   Right margin

Applying indents to paragraphs

Paragraphs can be indented from within the Paragraph dialog, or (to a lesser extent) by using the toolbar (if you add extra buttons to it).

Indenting text (1)

First, select the paragraph you want to indent. Pull down the Format menu and click Paragraph. Now follow step 1 below. If you want a left indent, carry out step 2. For a right indent, follow step 3. To achieve a first-line or hanging indent, follow step 4. Finally, irrespective of the indent type, carry out step 5.

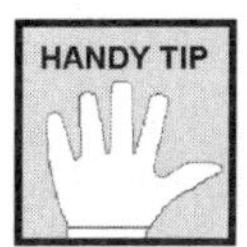

Re step 4 - to implement a hanging indent, type in a negative value e.g. -0.35, and the equivalent value in the Left field (e.g. 0.35).

Ensure the Indents and Alignment tab is active

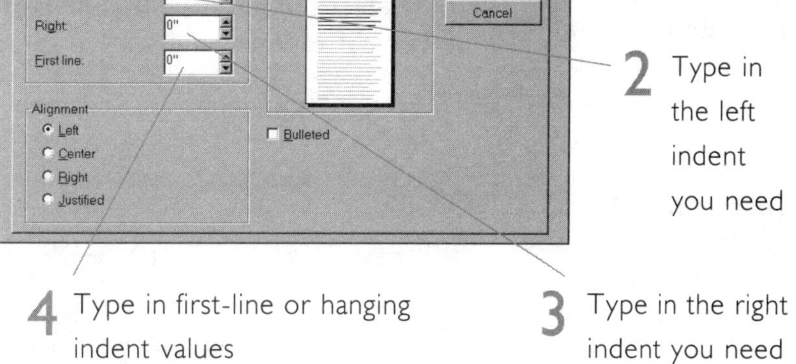

5 Click here

2 Type in the left indent you need

4 Type in first-line or hanging indent values

3 Type in the right indent you need

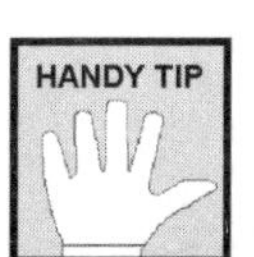

These buttons can be found within the Format category, in the Customize Works Toolbar dialog.

Using the toolbar to apply effects

As it ships, the Works toolbar *won't* let you indent text. However, you can add the following buttons:

Moves the indent out one level

Moves the indent in one level

For how to do this, see the 'The Works toolbar (2)' topic in Section 1.

Aligning paragraphs

You can use the following types of alignment:

Left

Text is flush with the left page margin.

Center

Text is aligned equidistantly between the left and right page margins.

Right

Text is flush with the right page margin.

Justified

Text is flush with the left *and* right page margins.

You can align text from within the Paragraph dialog, or (to a lesser extent) with the use of the toolbar.

Aligning text (1)

First, select the paragraph you want to indent. Pull down the Format menu and click Paragraph. Now:

You can only use the toolbar to apply full justification if you add a special button - 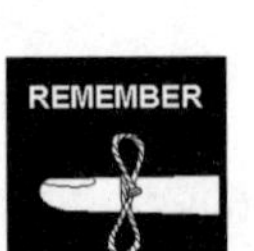 **- to it. This is found in the Format category within the Customize Works Toolbar dialog. See the 'The Works toolbar (2)' topic in Section 1.**

Ensure the Indents and Alignment tab is active

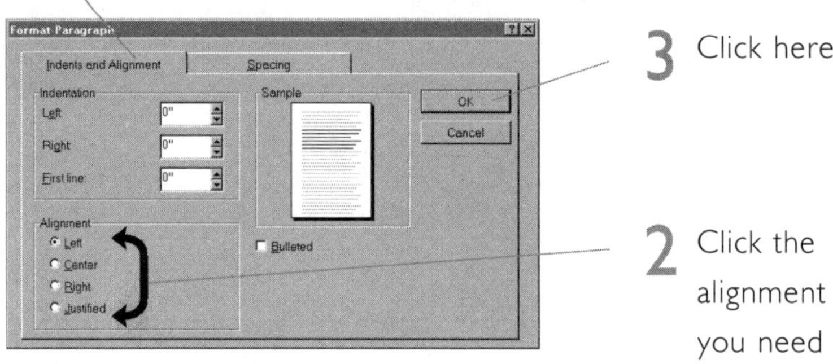

3 Click here

2 Click the alignment you need

If the toolbar isn't currently visible, pull down the View menu and click Toolbar.

Aligning text (2)

Select the relevant paragraph(s). Then click any of these:

Left align   Right align

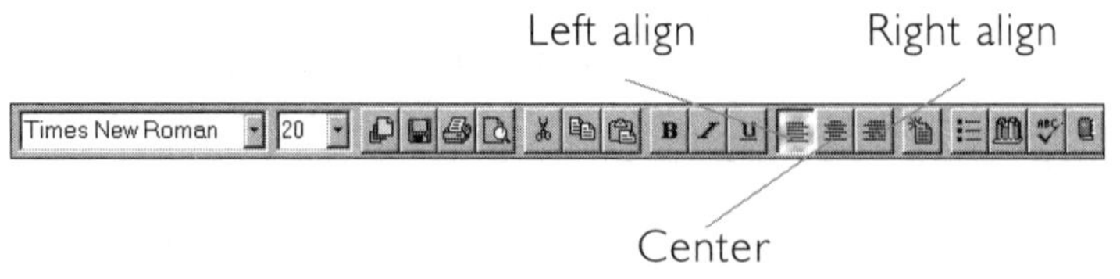

Specifying paragraph spacing

You can customise the vertical space before and/or after specific text paragraphs.

As a general rule, set low paragraph spacing settings: a little goes a long way.

By default, Works defines paragraph spacing in terms of lines, e.g. '6li' (6 lines). However, if you want you can enter measurements in different units. To do this, apply any of the following suffixes to values you enter:

- in – for inches e.g. '2 in'

- cm – for centimetres e.g. '5 cm'

- pt – for points e.g. '14 pt'

Points are a unit in typography: 72 points are roughly equivalent to one inch. The Word Processor also uses points to measure type sizes.

Applying paragraph spacing (1)

First, select the paragraph whose spacing you want to adjust. Pull down the Format menu and click Paragraph. Now carry out the steps below:

1 Ensure the Spacing tab is active

4 Click here

3 Type in the amount of post-paragraph spacing you need

2 Type in the amount of pre-paragraph spacing you need

Line spacing - an overview

It's often necessary to amend line spacing. This is the vertical distance between individual lines of text, or more accurately between the baseline (the imaginary line on which text appears to sit) of one line and the baseline of the previous.

The Word Processor lets you apply the following line spacing setting:

Auto

Each line is as high as the tallest character in it.

Alternatively, you can:

- specify the number of lines which should be applied as the line spacing (e.g. 4li - four lines).

- specify a number followed by a measurement in inches, centimetres or points (e.g. '0.5 in', '3 cm' or '12 pt').

Line spacing is also known as leading (pronounced 'ledding').

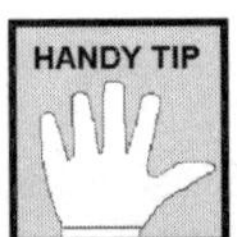

You can use these keyboard shortcuts to adjust line spacing: Ctrl+1, single spacing; Ctrl+5, l.5 spacing; Ctrl+2, double spacing.

This paragraph is in single line spacing. Newspapers frequently use this.

This paragraph is in 1½ line spacing. Probably no one uses this, but it serves as a useful illustration.

This paragraph is in double line spacing; writers use this when preparing manuscripts

Single line spacing

1.5 line spacing

Double line spacing

Adjusting line spacing

First, select the relevant paragraph(s). Then pull down the Format menu and do the following:

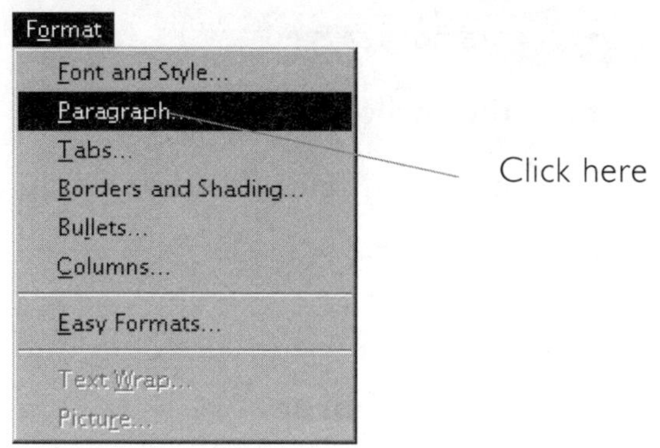

Click here

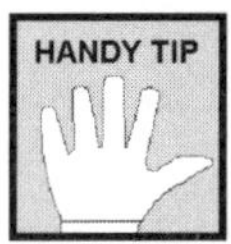

If you've just created a new document, you can set the line spacing before you begin to enter text. Simply leave the insertion point at the start of the document, and then follow the procedures outlined here.

Now perform steps 1 to 3 below:

1 Ensure the Spacing tab is active

3 Click here

2 Type in Auto, or the amount of line spacing you need

These buttons can be found within the Format category in the Customize Works Toolbar dialog. For how to implement these buttons, see the 'The Works toolbar (2)' topic in Section 1.

A shortcut...

As it ships, the Works toolbar *won't* let you adjust paragraph spacing. However, you can add buttons for the following functions easily and quickly:

  Single line spacing

 Double line spacing

Paragraph borders

By default, the Word Processor does not border paragraph text. However, you can apply a wide selection of borders if you want. You can specify:

- the border type

- the border thickness

- how many sides the border should have

- the border colour

- whether the bordered text should have a drop shadow

Applying a border

First, select the paragraph(s) you want to border. Then pull down the Format menu and click Borders and Shading. Now do the following:

The Sample area displays a preview of what your border combination will look like.

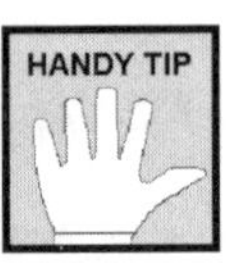

Re step 4 - click Outline to have all 4 sides bordered. Or click Outline with shadow to impose a drop shadow, too. Then proceed as normal.

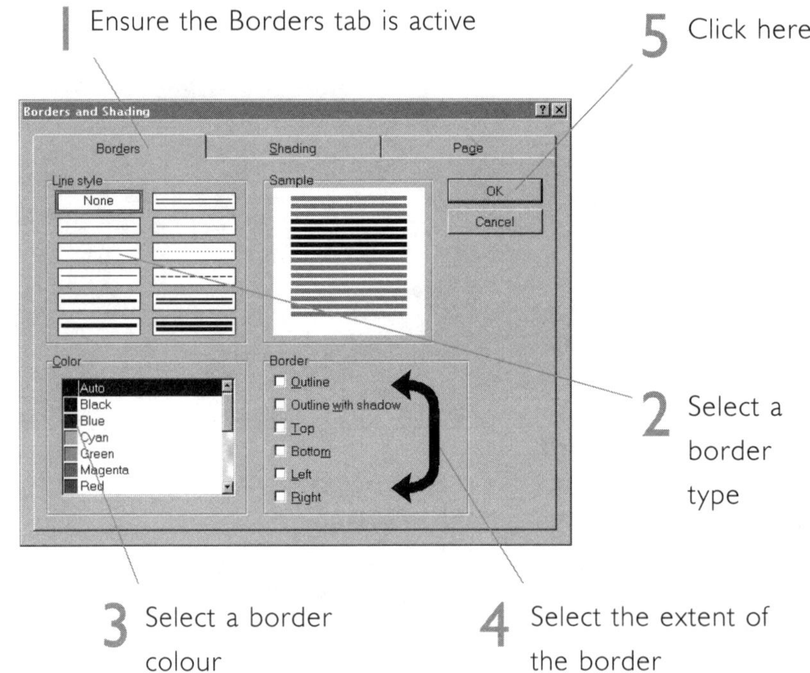

Paragraph fills

By default, the Word Processor does not apply a fill to text paragraphs. However, you can do the following if you want:

- apply a simple fill, if required

- apply a simple pattern, if required

- specify the foreground fill colour

- specify the background fill colour

Applying a fill

First, select the paragraph(s) you want to fill. Then pull down the Format menu and click Borders and Shading. Now carry out step 1 below. Follow steps 2, 3 or 4 as appropriate. Finally, carry out step 5:

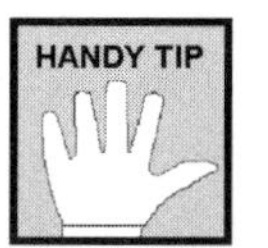

The Sample area displays a preview of what your fill combination will look like.

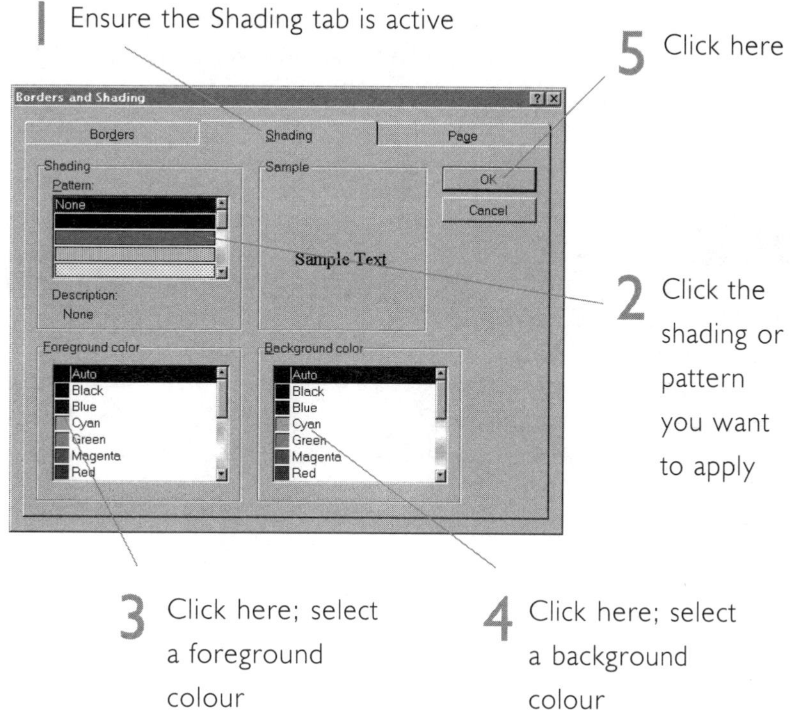

Ensure the Shading tab is active

5 Click here

2 Click the shading or pattern you want to apply

3 Click here; select a foreground colour

4 Click here; select a background colour

Working with tabs

Tabs are a means of indenting the first line of text paragraphs (you can also use indents for this purpose).

When you press the Tab key while the text insertion point is at the start of a paragraph, the text in the first line jumps to the next tab stop. This is a useful way to increase the legibility of your text. The Word Processor lets you set tab stops with great precision.

By default, tab stops are inserted automatically every half an inch. If you want, however, you can enter new or revised tab stop positions individually.

Never use the Space Bar to indent paragraphs: spaces vary in size according to the typeface and type size applying to specific paragraphs.

Setting tab stops

First, select the paragraph(s) in which you need to set tab stops. Pull down the Format menu and click Tabs. Now carry out step 1 below. If you want to implement a new default tab stop position, follow step 2. If you need to set up individual tab stops, carry out steps 3 and 4 as often as necessary. Finally, follow step 5 to confirm your changes.

When you've performed steps 3 & 4, the individual tab stop position appears here:

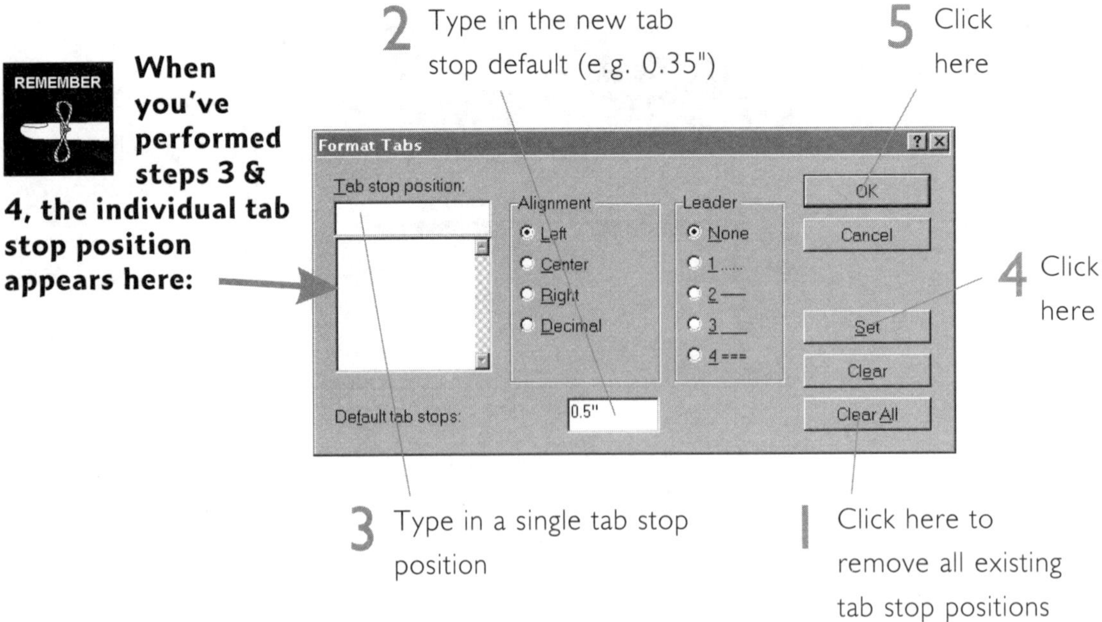

Microsoft Works in easy steps

Searching for text

The Works wildcard is very useful: it stands for *any* character. For instance, searching for 'me?t' would find 'meet' or 'meat'. See 'Entering codes' below for more information.

The Word Processor lets you search for specific text within the active document.

You can also search for special characters. For example, you can look for paragraph marks, tabs, wildcards, question marks, page breaks and spaces.

You can also:

- limit the search to words which match the case of the text you specify (e.g. if you search for 'Arm', Works will not flag 'arm' or 'ARM')

- limit the search to whole words (e.g. if you search for 'eat', Works will not flag 'beat' or 'meat')

Initiating a text search

Pull down the Edit menu and click Find. Now do the following:

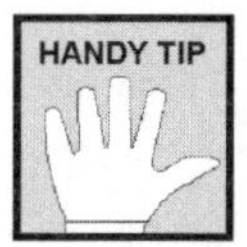

You can use a keyboard shortcut to launch the Find dialog: simply press Ctrl+F.

1 Type in the text you want to find

3 Click here to start the search

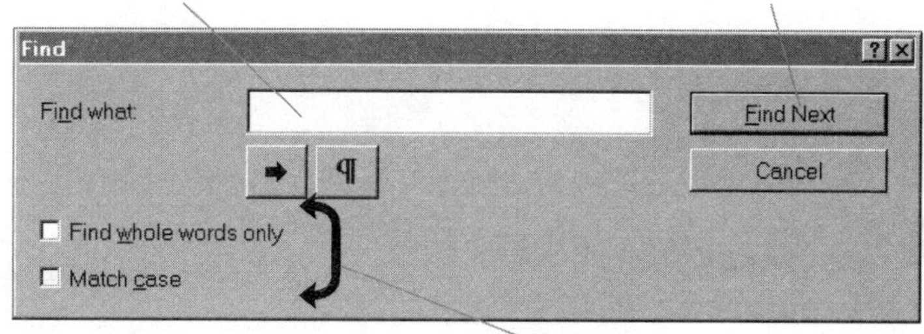

2 Specify the search parameters you need

Entering codes

When you complete step 1, you can enter the following:

^w	Space	^d	Page break
^t	Tab	?	Wildcard
^p	Paragraph mark	^?	Question mark

Replacing text

When you've located text, you can have the Word Processor replace it automatically with the text of your choice.

You can customise find-and-replace operations with the same parameters as a simple Find operation. For example, you can make them case-specific, or only replace whole words. You can also incorporate a variety of codes (for how to do this, see the 'Searching for text' topic on the previous page.

There is, however, one exception to this: for obvious reasons, wildcards can't be incorporated in replacement text.

Initiating a find-and-replace operation

First pull down the Edit menu and click Replace. Now follow steps 1 and 2 below. Carry out step 3, as appropriate. Finally, follow step 4 (or see the associated tip):

You can use a keyboard shortcut here: simply press Ctrl+H.

If you don't want *all* instances of the text replaced immediately, don't carry out step 4. Instead, click the Find Next button after step 3. When the first match has been found, click Replace. Repeat this as often as necessary.

1 Type in the text you want to find

2 Type in the replacement text

4 Click here to replace all instances of the text

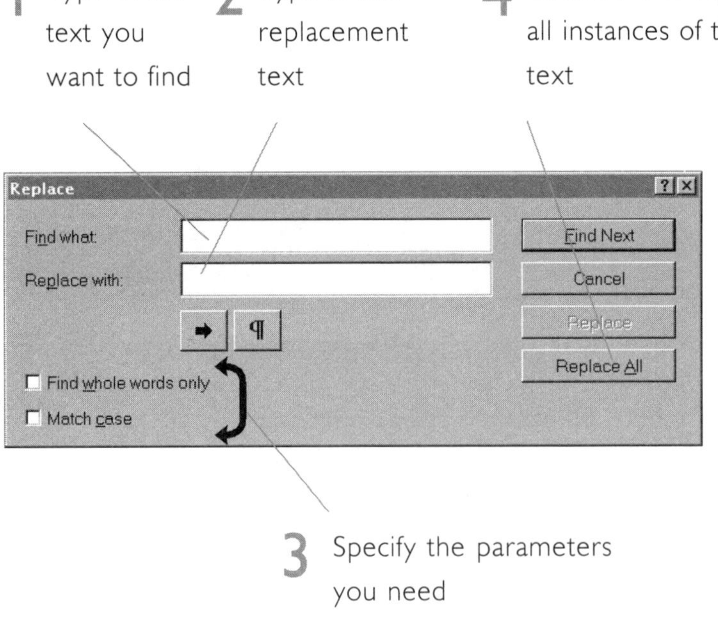

3 Specify the parameters you need

Working with headers

To edit an *existing* header, simply follow the procedures outlined here; in step 1, amend the current header text as necessary.

You can have the Word Processor print text at the top of each page within a document; the area of the page where repeated text appears is called the 'header'. In the same way, you can have text printed at the base of each page; in this case, the relevant page area is called the 'footer'. Headers and footers are printed within the top and bottom page margins, respectively.

Inserting a header

In Normal view, move to the top of the first page, then click in the Header (H) area. Alternatively, in Page Layout view move to the top of the relevant page and click in the Header area.

Now do the following:

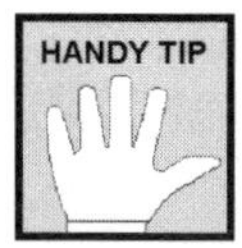

Re step 1 - you can have the Word Processor insert a special code which automatically inserts the page number in the header. To do this, pull down the Insert menu and click Page Number.

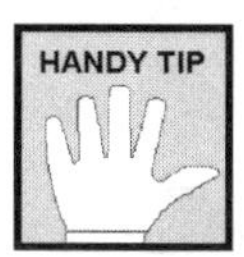

Header text can be formatted in the normal way. For instance, you can apply a new font and/or type size.

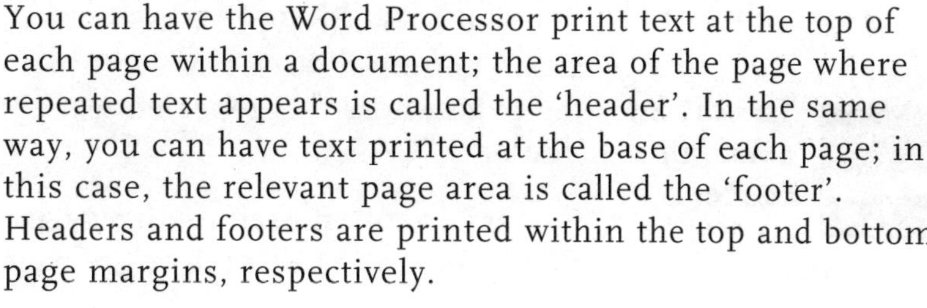

Type in the Header text

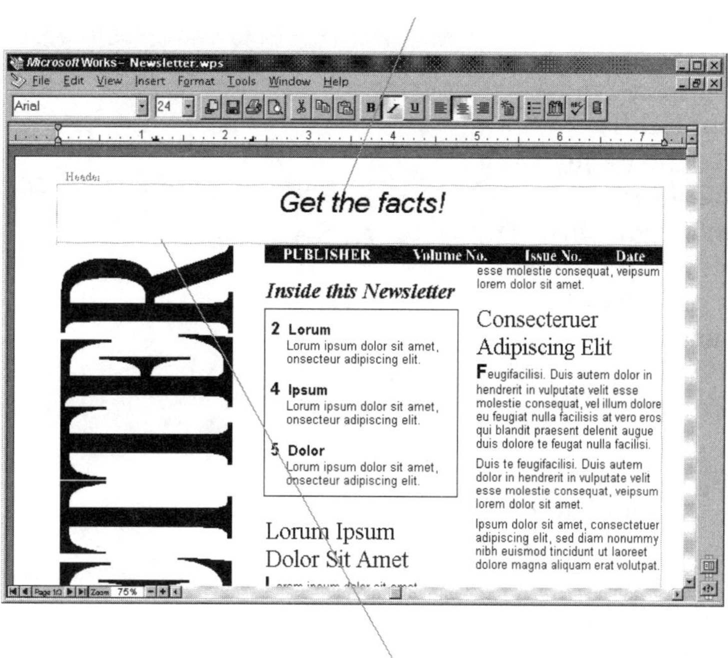

The Header area in
Page Layout view

Working with footers

To edit an *existing* footer, simply follow the procedures outlined here; in step 1, amend the current footer text as necessary.

You can have the Word Processor automatically print text at the bottom of each page within a document. The area of the page where this repeated text appears is called the 'footer'.

Footers are often used to display an abbreviated version of the document's title and/or the page number.

Inserting a footer

In Normal view, move to the top of the first page then click in the Footer (F) area. Alternatively, in Page Layout view move to the bottom of the relevant page and click in the Footer area.

Then do the following:

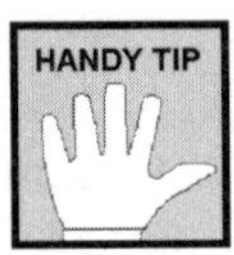

Re step 1 - you can have the Word Processor insert a special code which automatically inserts the page number in the footer. To do this, pull down the Insert menu and click Page Number.

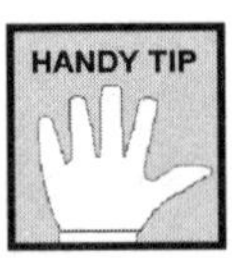

Footer text can be formatted in the normal way. For instance, you can apply a new font and/or type size.

Type in the Footer text

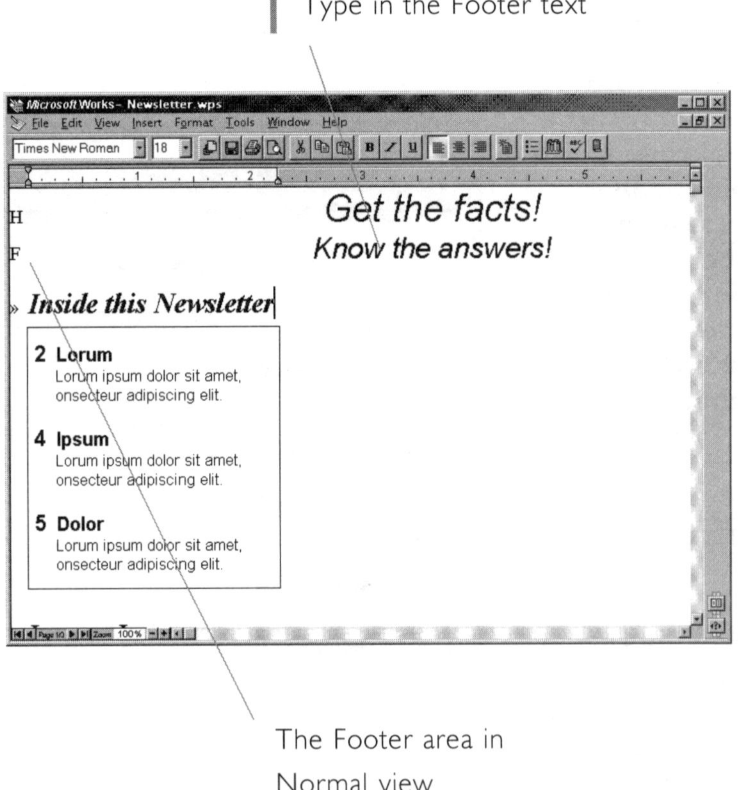

The Footer area in Normal view

Undo and redo

You can only use Undo and Redo *immediately* **after you've initiated an editing or formatting operation.**

The Word Processor lets you reverse – 'undo' – just about any editing operation. If, in the event, you decide that you do want to proceed with an operation which you've reversed, you can 'redo' it. In effect, this amounts to undoing an undo.

You can undo and redo actions in the following ways (in descending order of complexity):

- via the keyboard

- from within the Edit menu

- from within the toolbar

The entry differs according to whether you're carrying out an undo or redo.

Using the keyboard
Simply press Ctrl+Z to undo an action. If you want to reinstate it immediately afterwards, press Ctrl+Z again.

Using the Edit menu
Pull down the Edit menu and do the following:

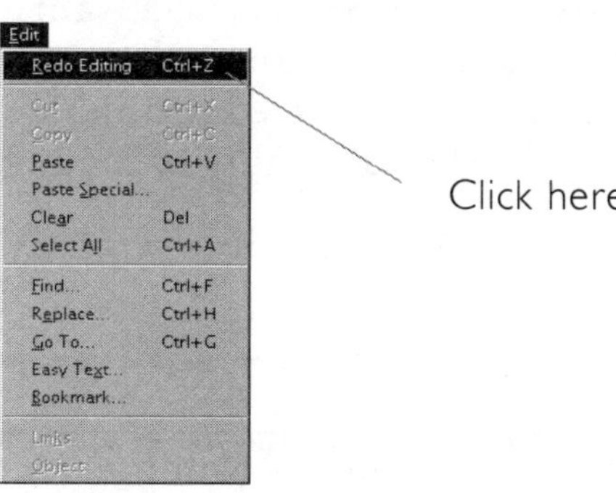

Click here

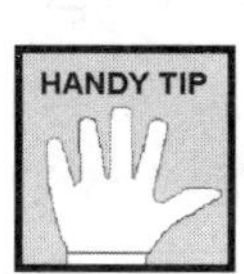

This button can be found within the Edit category in the Customize Works Toolbar dialog. For how to add this button to your toolbar, see the 'The Works toolbar (2)' topic in Section 1.

Using the toolbar
As it ships, the Works toolbar *won't* let you undo or redo operations. However, you can add the following button easily and quickly:

Undo/redo button

Easy Formats - an overview

The Word Processor module comes with a selection of pre-defined Easy Formats. Examples are:

- Boxed text

- Contemporary masthead

- Coupon

- Cursive note

- Flyer text

- Hanging indent

- List with lines

- Quotation

- Title page

Easy Formats are named collections of associated formatting commands. The advantage of using Easy Formats is that you can apply more than one formatting enhancement to selected text in one go. Another advantage is the professional quality of the results.

You can easily create your own Easy Formats for later use.

REMEMBER

An example of an Easy Format - this is the 'Contemporary masthead' Easy Format applied to part of a document created with the Letterhead TaskWizard.

Header

Company Name

Address Line 1
Address Line 2
City, Postal Code, County
Country

Phone 555-1234
Fax 555-9876

30 January 1996

Name
Address
City, County, Postal Code

Dear John,

Start typing your letter here.

Creating an Easy Format

The easiest way to create an Easy Format is to:

1. apply the appropriate formatting enhancements to specific text and then select it

2. tell Works to save this formatting as an Easy Format

First, carry out step 1 above. Then pull down the Format menu and click Easy Formats. Now do the following:

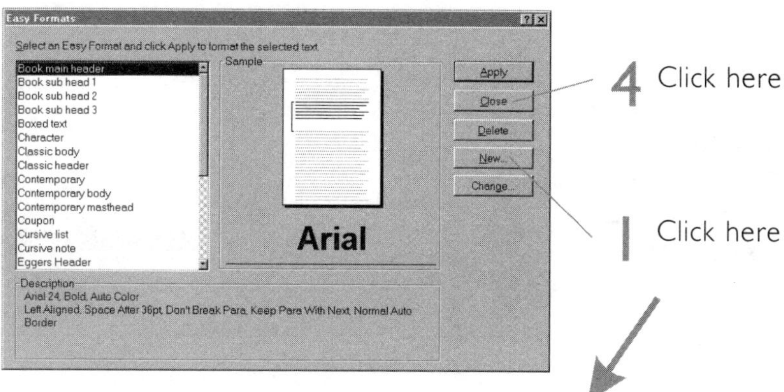

4 Click here

1 Click here

If you want to adjust the formatting of your new Easy Format, click any of these buttons (after step 2). Complete the dialog which launches in the normal way. Finally, carry out steps 3 and 4.

2 Type in a name for your Easy Format

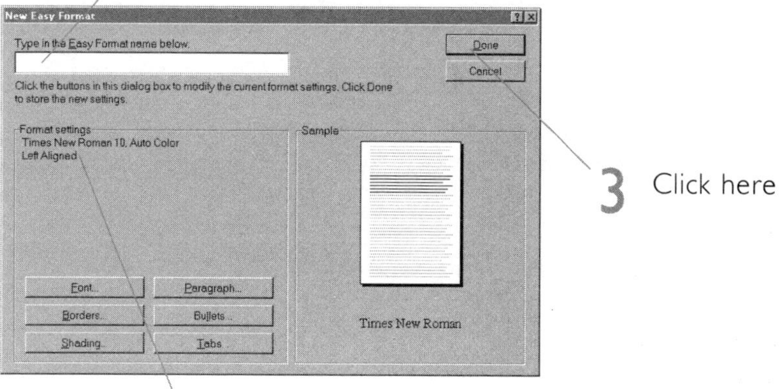

3 Click here

Brief description of formatting associated with the new Easy Format

See 'Applying an Easy Format' to use your new format.

Applying an Easy Format

Applying Easy Formats is easy.

First, select the text you want to apply the Easy Format to. Or, if you only want to apply it to a single paragraph, place the insertion point inside it. Pull down the Format menu and click Easy Formats. Now do the following:

Click the Easy Format you want to apply

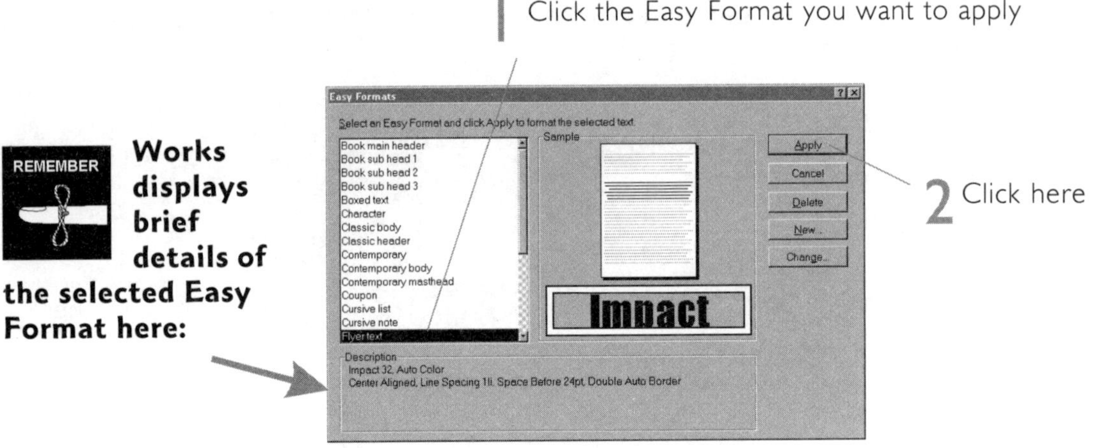

2 Click here

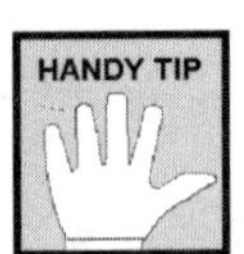

Works displays brief details of the selected Easy Format here:

Shortcut for applying Easy Formats

Works makes it even easier to apply Easy Formats if you currently have the toolbar on-screen (if you haven't, pull down the View menu and click Toolbar).

If the Easy Format you want to apply isn't listed, click More Easy Formats in the menu. This launches the Easy Formats dialog. Complete this in line with the instructions above.

Select the text you want to apply the format to. Then do the following:

Click here

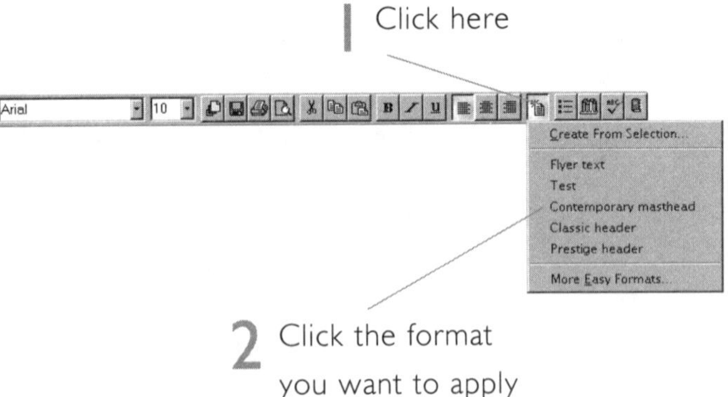

2 Click the format you want to apply

Amending an Easy Format

You can easily adjust the formatting associated with existing Easy Formats.

Pull down the Format menu and click Easy Formats. Now carry out the following steps:

1 Select the Easy Format you want to amend

6 Click here

2 Click here

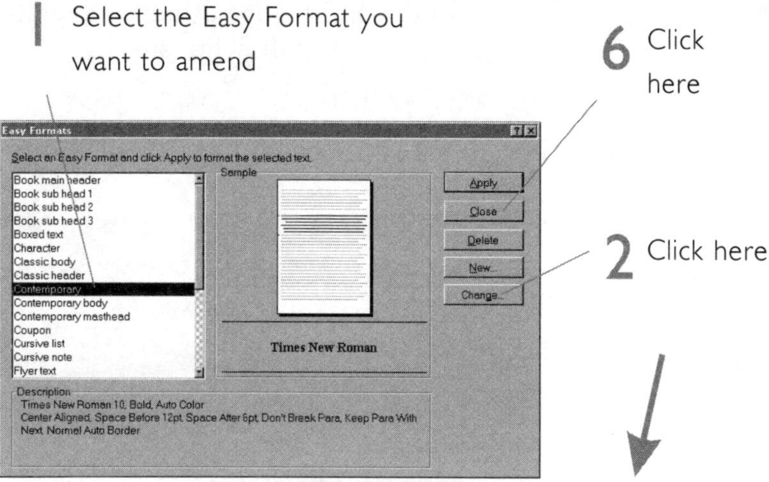

3 Rename the Easy Format, if required

5 Click here

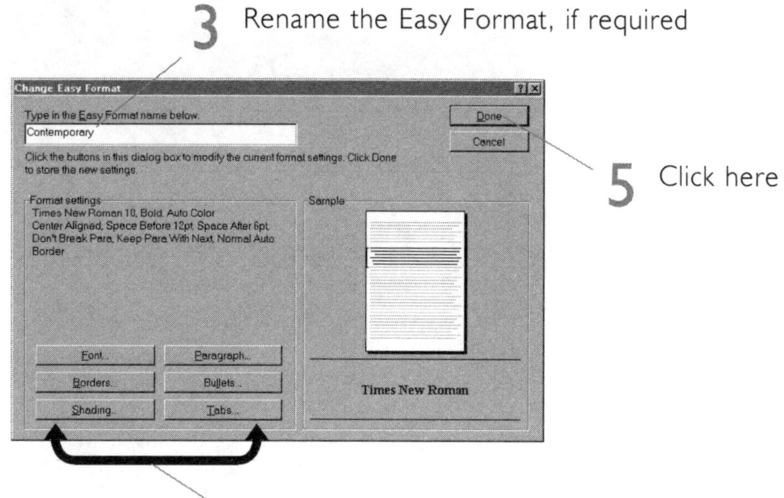

4 Click any of these buttons; complete the dialog which launches in the normal way.

Deleting Easy Formats

Good housekeeping sometimes makes it necessary to remove unwanted Easy Formats (after all, there's no point retaining an Easy Format if you're never likely to use it). The Word Processor lets you do this very easily.

Removing an Easy Format

Pull down the Format menu and click Easy Formats. Now carry out the following steps:

Click the format you want to remove

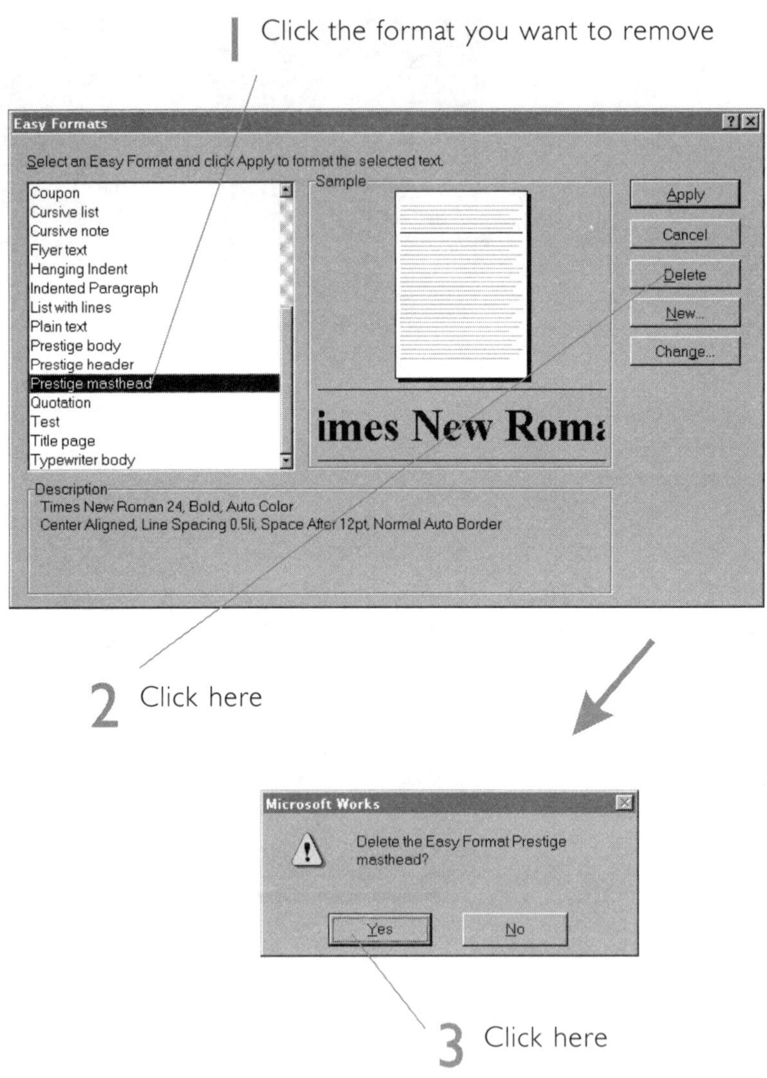

2 Click here

3 Click here

Spell-checking text

You can check for a variety of errors: misspellings; incorrect capitalisations (e.g. 'THis' at the start of a sentence); repeated words (e.g. 'the the').

Works makes use of two separate dictionaries. One can be thought of as *yours*. When you follow step 4, the flagged word is stored in this and recognised in future checking sessions.

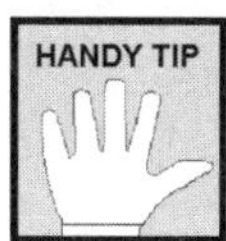

If the flagged word isn't correct and Works' suggestions are also wrong, type in the correct version in the Change To field. Then carry out step 2 or 3.

To check all the text within the active document in one go, pull down the Tools menu and click Spelling. Works starts spell-checking the document from the beginning. When it encounters a word it doesn't recognise, Works flags it and produces a special dialog (see below). Usually, it provides alternative suggestions; if one of these is correct, you can opt to have it replace the flagged word. You can do this singly (i.e. just this instance is replaced) or globally (where all future instances – within the current checking session – are replaced).

Alternatively, you can have Works:

- ignore *this* instance of the flagged word & resume checking

- ignore *all* future instances of the word & resume checking

- add the word to your personal dictionary & resume checking

Carry out step 1 below. Then follow step 2 or 3, or any one of steps 4, 5 or 6.

1 If one of the suggestions here is correct, click it, then follow step 2 or 3

5 Click here to ignore just this instance

6 Click here to ignore all future instances

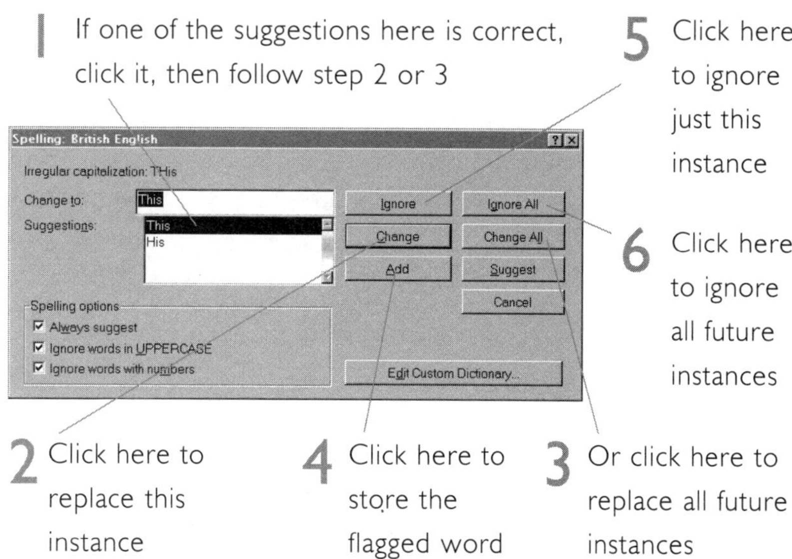

2 Click here to replace this instance

4 Click here to store the flagged word

3 Or click here to replace all future instances

Searching for synonyms

The Word Processor lets you search for synonyms while you're editing the active document. You do this by calling up the resident thesaurus. The thesaurus categorises words into meanings, and each meaning is allocated various synonyms from which you can choose.

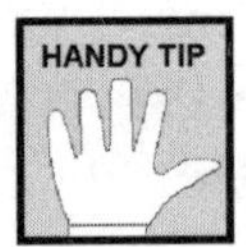

You can also use a keyboard shortcut to launch the thesaurus: simply press Shift+F7.

As a bonus, the thesaurus also supplies antonyms. For example, if you look up 'good' in the thesaurus, Works lists 'abominable', 'bad', 'base', 'corrupt' etc. as antonyms.

Using the thesaurus

First, select the word for which you require a synonym or antonym (or simply position the insertion point within it). Pull down the Tools menu and click Thesaurus. Now do the following:

The selected word appears here

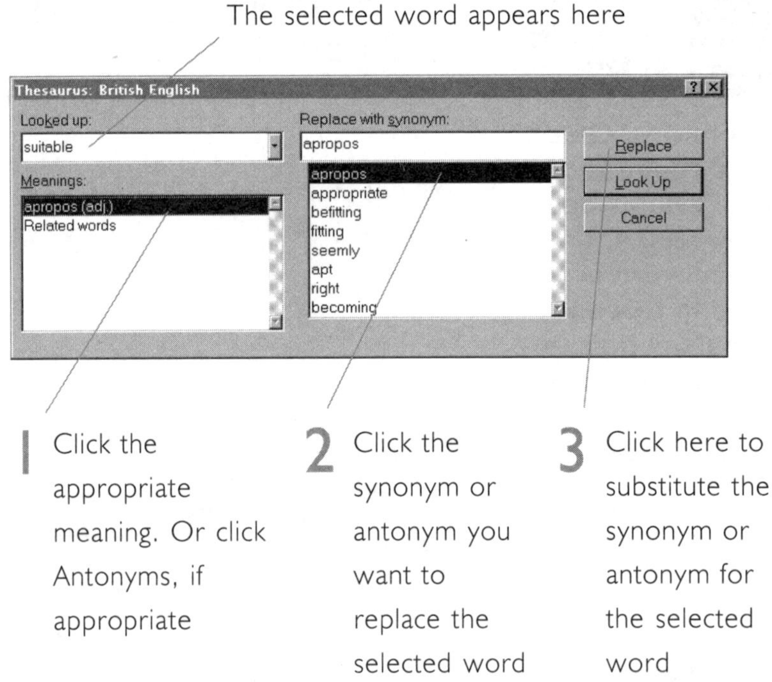

1 Click the appropriate meaning. Or click Antonyms, if appropriate

2 Click the synonym or antonym you want to replace the selected word

3 Click here to substitute the synonym or antonym for the selected word

Working with pictures

The Word Processor module lets you add colour or greyscale pictures to the active document. Pictures – also called graphics – include:

- drawings produced in other programs

- clip art

- scanned photographs

Use pictures – whatever their source – to add much needed visual impact to documents. But use them judiciously: too much colour can be off-putting, and ultimately self-defeating.

Pictures are stored in various third-party formats. These formats are organised into two basic types:

Bitmap images

Bitmaps consist of pixels (dots) arranged in such a way that they form a graphic image. Because of the very nature of bitmaps, the question of 'resolution' – the sharpness of an image expressed in dpi (dots per inch) – is very important. Bitmaps look best if they're displayed at their native resolution. Works can manipulate a wide variety of third-party bitmap graphics formats. These include: PCX, TIF, TGA and GIF.

Vector images

You can also insert vector graphics files into Word Processor documents. Vector images consist of and are defined by algebraic equations. They're less complex than bitmaps: they contain less detail. Vector files can also include bitmap information.

Irrespective of the format type, Works can incorporate pictures with the help of special 'filters'. These are special mini-programs whose job it is to translate third-party formats into a form which Works can use.

Brief notes on picture formats

Graphics formats Works will accept include the following (the column on the left shows the relevant file suffix):

CGM — Computer Graphics Metafile. A vector format frequently used in the past, especially as a medium for clip-art transmission. Less often used nowadays.

EPS — Encapsulated PostScript. Perhaps the most widely used PostScript format. PostScript combines vector *and* bitmap data very successfully. Incorporates a low-resolution bitmap 'header' for preview purposes.

GIF — Graphics Interchange Format. Developed for the on-line transmission of graphics data across the CompuServe network. Just about any Windows program – and a lot more besides – will read GIF. Disadvantage: it can't handle more than 256 colours. Compression is supported.

PCD — (Kodak) PhotoCD. Used primarily to store photographs on CD.

PCX — An old standby. Originated with PC Paintbrush, a paint program. Used for years to transfer graphics data between Windows applications.

TGA — Targa. A high-end format, and also a bridge with so-called low-end computers (e.g. Amiga and Atari). Often used in PC and Mac paint and ray-tracing programs because of its high-resolution colour fidelity.

TIFF — Tagged Image File Format. Suffix: .TIF. If anything, even more widely used than PCX, across a whole range of platforms and applications.

Inserting pictures

You insert pictures into the Word Processor via the ClipArt Gallery. This provides a visual catalogue of pictures on your system, and is a useful springboard for keeping track of them.

First, position the insertion point at the location within the active document where you want to insert the picture. Pull down the Insert menu and do the following:

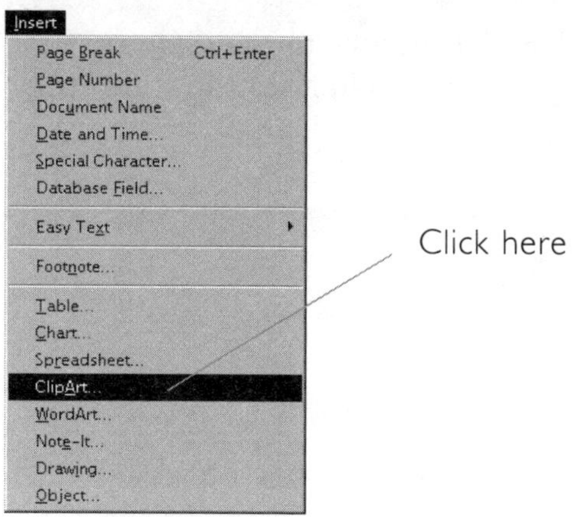

Click here

Now carry out the following steps:

2 Click the image you want to insert

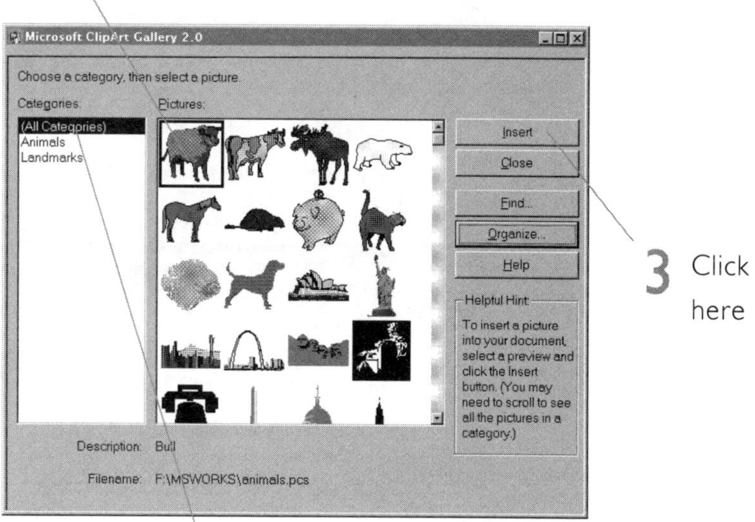

3 Click here

Click the relevant category

Adding an image to the Gallery

You can easily add additional images to the ClipArt Gallery. When you do this, you're simply telling the Gallery (since it's purely an organisational aid) where the picture files are.

To add a picture to the Gallery, first launch it in the normal way. Then do the following:

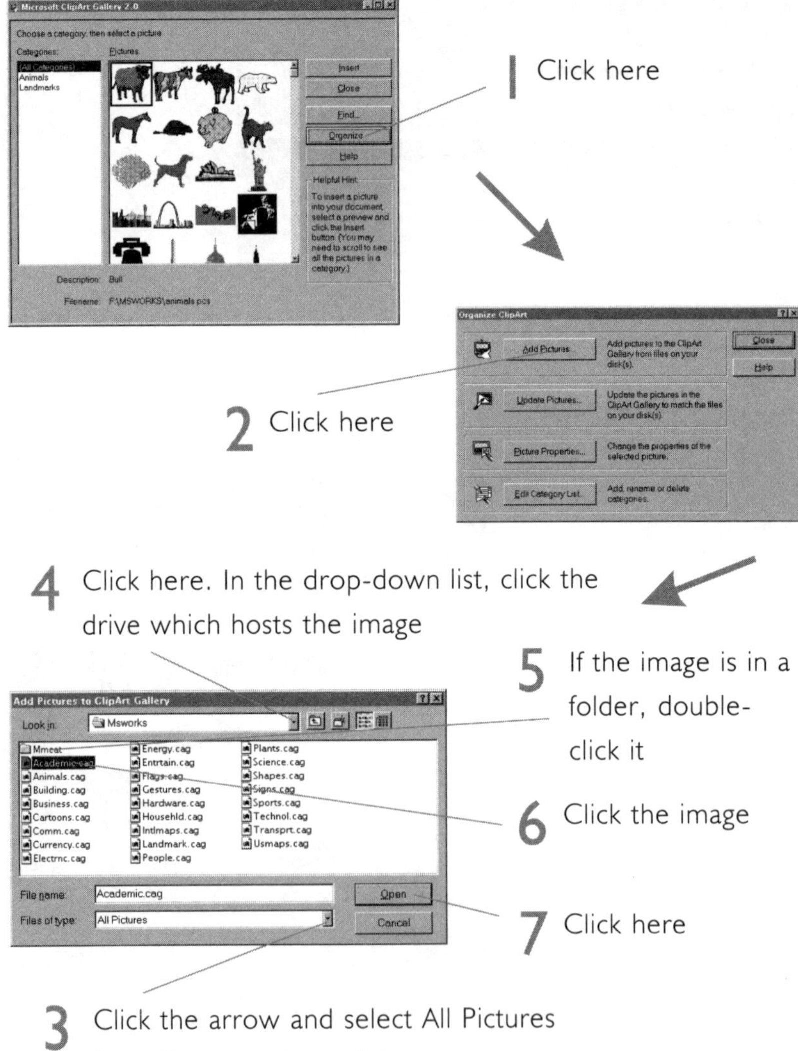

Manipulating pictures - an overview

Once you've inserted pictures into a Word Processor document, you can amend them in a variety of ways. You can:

- rescale them

- apply a border

- move them

Selecting an image

To carry out any of these operations, you have to select the relevant picture first. To do this, simply position the mouse pointer over the image and left-click once. Works surrounds the image with eight handles. These are positioned at the four corners, and midway on each side. The illustration below demonstrates these:

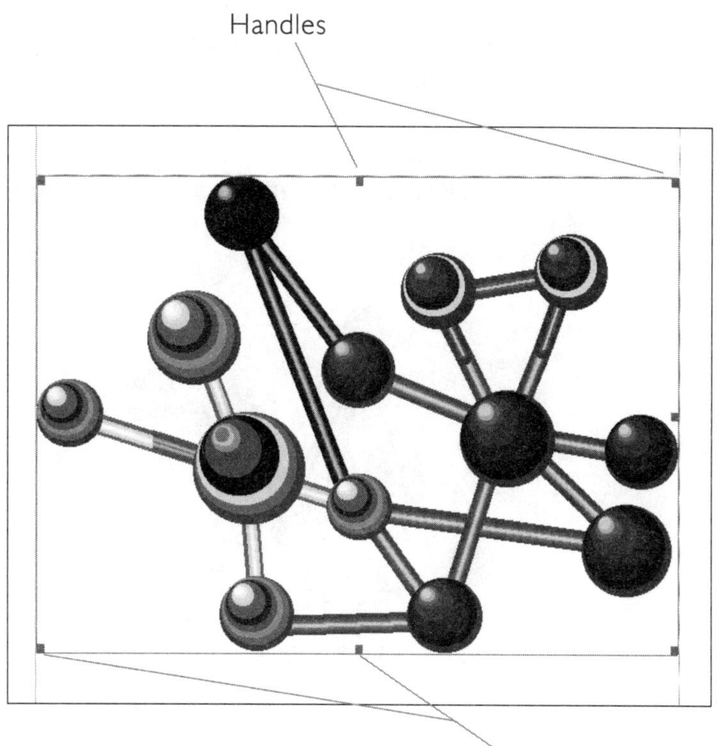

Rescaling pictures

There are two ways in which you can rescale pictures:

- proportionally, where the height/width ratio remains constant

- disproportionately, where the height/width ratio is disrupted (this is sometimes called 'warping' or 'skewing')

To rescale a picture, first select it. Then move the mouse pointer over:

- one of the corner handles, if you want to rescale the image proportionally,

or

- one of the handles in the middle of the sides, if you want to warp it

In either eventuality, the mouse pointer changes to a double-headed arrow and the word 'RESIZE' appears below it. Click and hold down the left mouse button. Drag outwards to increase the image size or inwards to decrease it. Release the mouse button to confirm the change.

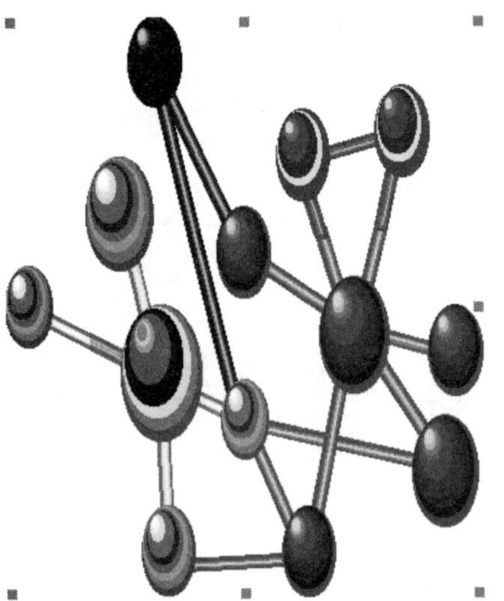

Here, the image from the previous page has been skewed from the right inwards

Bordering pictures

By default, the Word Processor does not apply a border to inserted pictures. However, you can apply a wide selection of borders if you want. You can specify:

- the border type

- the border thickness

- how many sides the border should have

- the border colour

- whether the bordered image should have a drop shadow

Applying a border

First, select the picture you want to border. Then pull down the Format menu and click Borders and Shading. Now do the following:

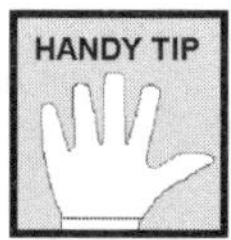

The Sample field provides a preview of what your border combination will look like.

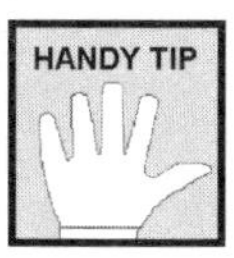

Re step 4 - click Outline to have all 4 sides bordered. Or click Outline with shadow to impose a drop shadow, too. Then proceed as normal.

Ensure the Borders tab is active

5 Click here

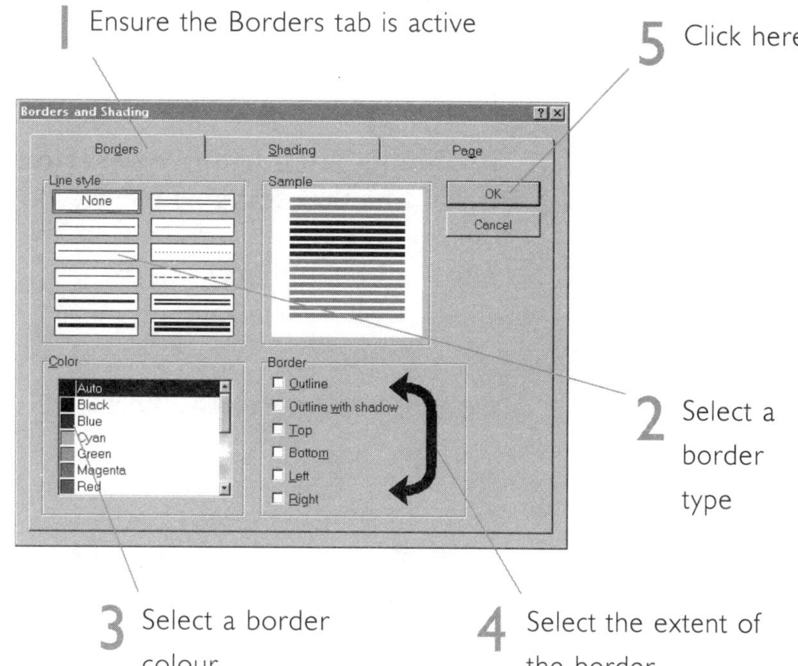

2 Select a border type

3 Select a border colour

4 Select the extent of the border

Moving pictures

You can easily move pictures from one location on the page to another.

First, click in the image to select it. Move the mouse pointer over it; it changes to a pointing arrow. Left-click once and hold down the button. Drag the picture to its new location (as you do so, the word 'MOVE' appears underneath the cursor).

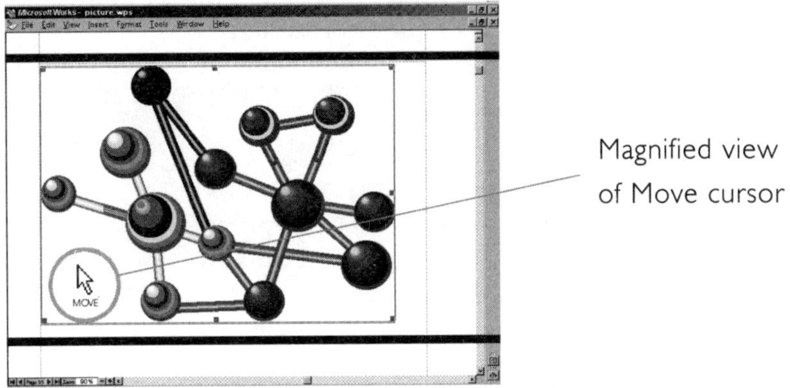

Magnified view of Move cursor

Release the mouse button to confirm the move.

Problems with Move operations?

If you find that dragging pictures has no effect, select the image. Pull down the Format menu and click Picture. Carry out the following steps:

Ensure the Text Wrap tab is active

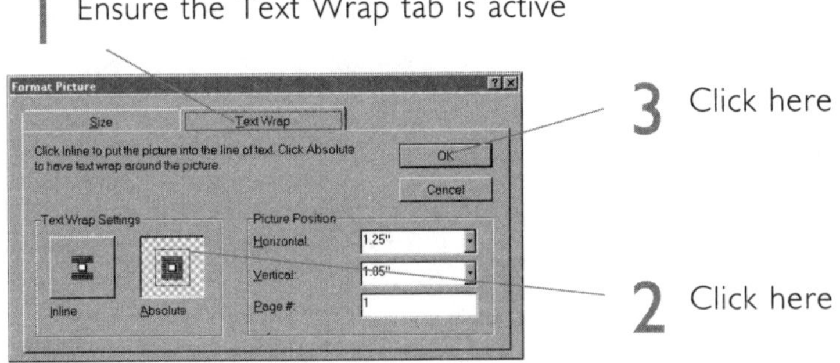

3 Click here

2 Click here

Now carry out the move again.

Page setup - an overview

You can control the following aspects of page layout in the Word Processor module:

- the top, bottom, left and/or right page margins

- the distance between the top page edge and the top edge of the header

- the distance between the bottom page edge and bottom edge of the footer

The illustration below shows these page components:

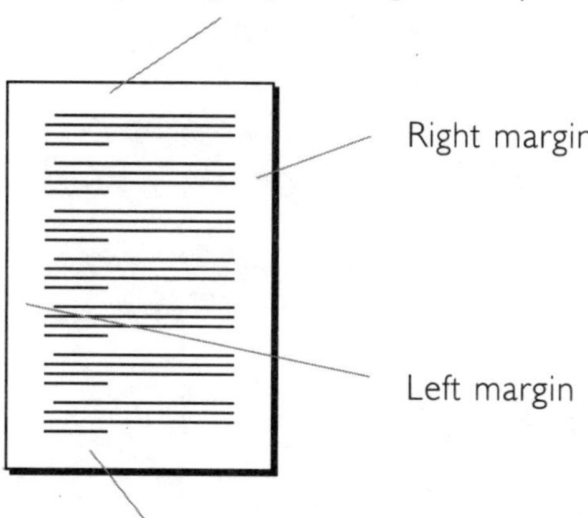

You can also specify:

- the overall page size (inclusive of margins and headers/footers)

- the page orientation ('landscape' or 'portrait')

If none of the supplied page sizes is suitable, you can even customise your own.

Specifying margins

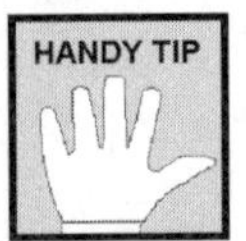

Margin settings are the framework on which indents and tabs are based.

All documents have margins, because printing on the whole of a sheet is both unsightly and – in the case of many printers, since the mechanism has to grip the page – impossible. Documents need a certain amount of 'white space' (the unprinted portion of the page) to balance the areas which contain text and graphics. Without this, they can't be visually effective.

As a result, it's important to set margins correctly. Fortunately, the Word Processor module makes the job of changing margin settings easy.

Customising margins

Pull down the File menu and click Page Setup. Now carry out step 1 below. Then follow steps 2 or 3, as appropriate. Finally, carry out step 4:

1 Ensure the Margins tab is active

4 Click here

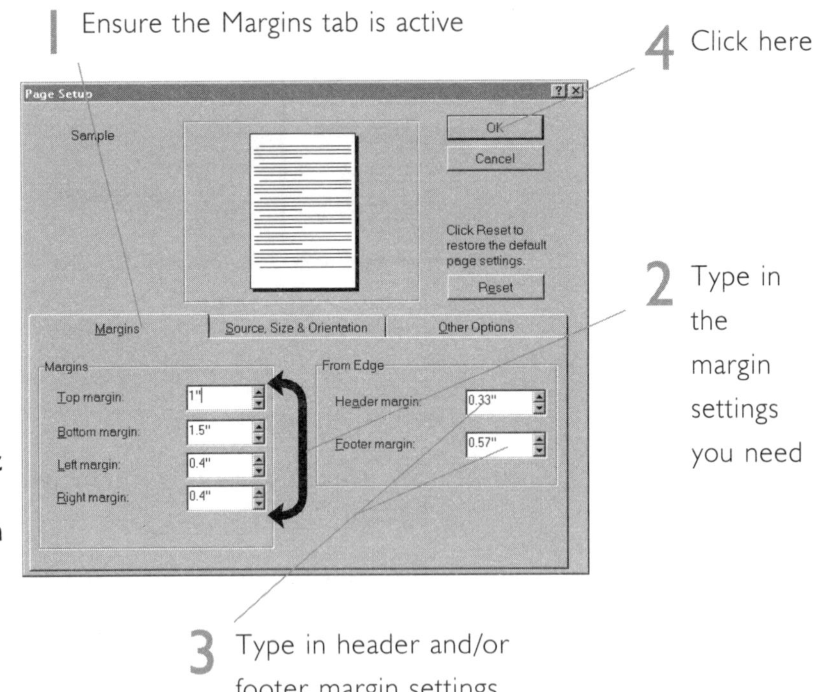

2 Type in the margin settings you need

You can only adjust margin settings on a document-wide basis (not for individual pages).

3 Type in header and/or footer margin settings

Specifying the page size

The Word Processor comes with 11 preset page sizes. These are suitable for most purposes. However, if you need to you can also set up your own page definition.

There are two aspects to every page size:

- a vertical measurement

- a horizontal measurement

There are two possible orientations:

Portrait   Landscape

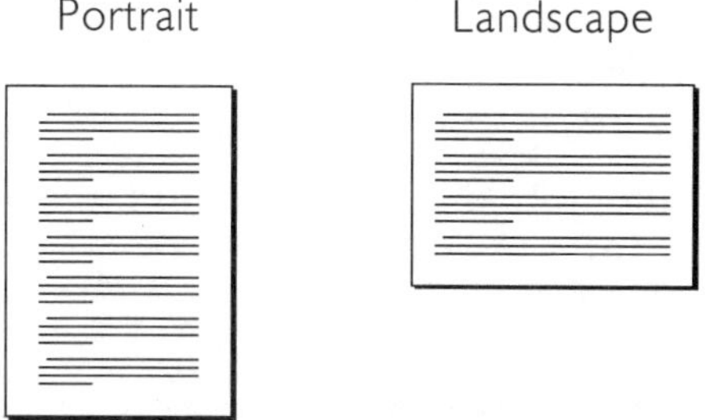

Setting the page size

First, position the insertion point at the location within the active document from which you want the new margin(s) to apply. Then pull down the File menu and click Page Setup. Now do the following:

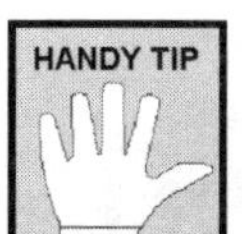

To create your own page size, click Custom Size in step 2. Then type in the appropriate measurements in the Width & Height fields. Finally, carry out step 4.

Ensure this tab is active

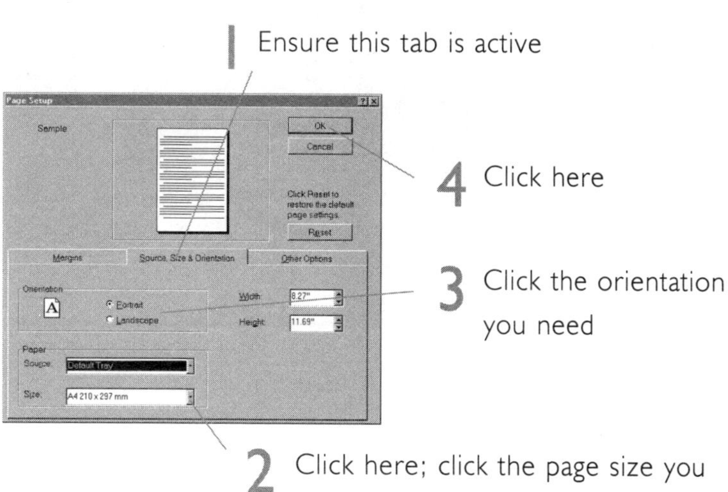

4 Click here

3 Click the orientation you need

2 Click here; click the page size you need in the drop-down list

Using Print Preview

The Word Processor provides a special view mode called Print Preview. This displays the active document (one page at a time) exactly as it will look when printed. Use Print Preview as a final check just before you print your document.

When you're using Print Preview, you can zoom in or out on the active page. What you can't do, however, is:

- display more than one page at a time

- edit or revise the active document (use Page Layout view instead)

Launching Print Preview

Pull down the File menu and click Print Preview. This is the result:

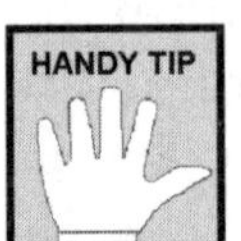

You can use a keyboard shortcut to leave Print Preview mode: simply press Esc.

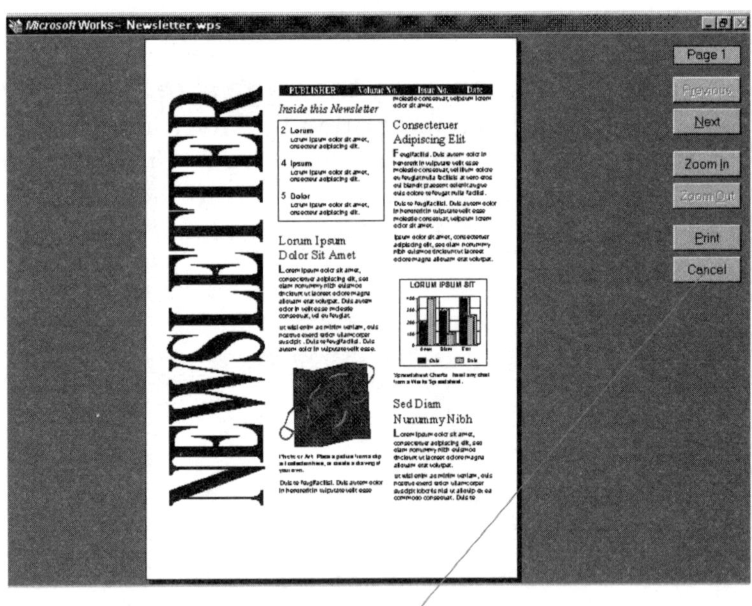

Click here to leave Print Preview and return to Normal or Page Layout view

Zooming in or out in Print Preview

There are two methods you can use here.

Using the mouse

Move the mouse pointer over the page area; it changes to a magnifying glass. Position this over the portion of the active document which you want to expand. Left-click once. Repeat this if necessary.

When you've reached the limit of magnification which Works supports, left-clicking with the mouse *decreases* the magnification.

A magnified view of part of the Print Preview screen

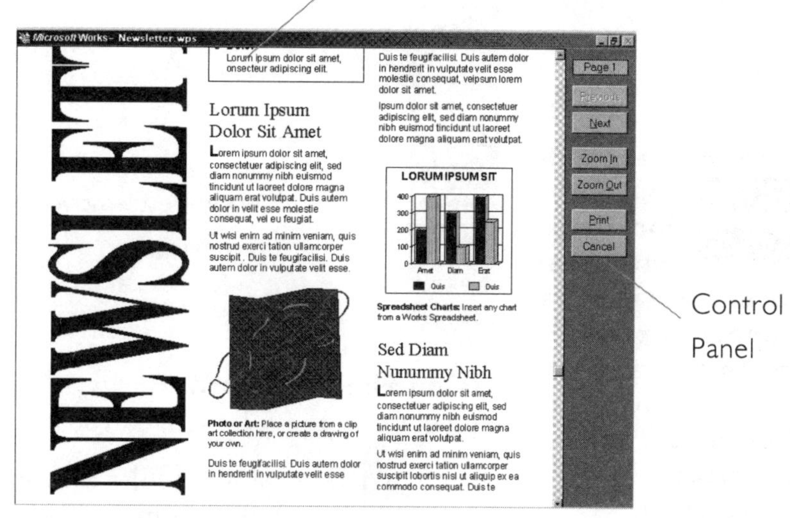

Control Panel

Depending on the current level of magnification, one of the Zoom buttons may be greyed out, and therefore unavailable.

Using the Control Panel

Launch Print Preview. Then carry out the following actions:

Click here to increase the magnification

Click here to decrease the magnification

Changing pages in Print Preview

Although you can only view one page at a time in Print Preview mode, you can step backwards and forwards through the document as often as necessary.

There are three methods you can use (in descending order of usefulness).

Using the Control Panel

Carry out the following actions:

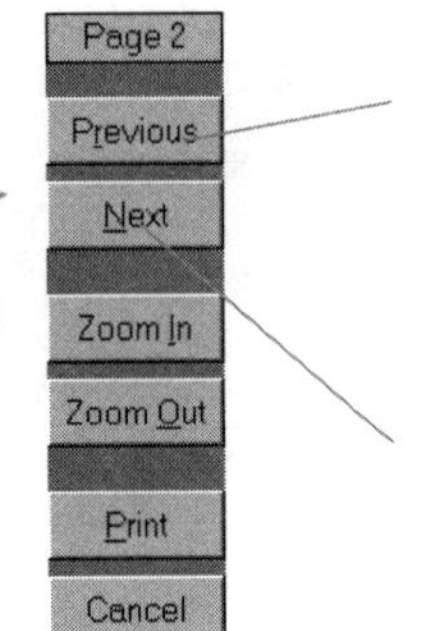

Click here to move to the previous page

Click here to move to the next page

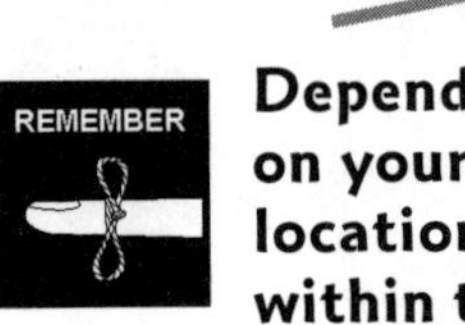

Depending on your location within the document (and the number of pages), one of these buttons may be greyed out, and therefore unavailable.

Using the keyboard

You can use the following keyboard shortcuts:

Page Up — Moves to the previous page (unavailable within a magnified page view)

Page Down — Moves to the next page (unavailable within a magnified page view)

Up cursor — Within a magnified view of a page, moves towards the top of the page

Down cursor — Within a magnified view of a page, moves towards the base of the page

Using the scroll bars

When you're working with a magnified view of a page, use the vertical and/or horizontal scroll bars (using the standard Windows techniques) to move up or down within the page.

Printer setup

The question of which printer you select affects how the document displays in Print Preview mode.

Most Word Processor documents need to be printed eventually. Before you can begin printing, however, you must ensure that:

- the correct printer is selected (if you have more than one installed)

- the correct printer settings are in force

Works calls these collectively the 'printer setup'.

Irrespective of the printer selected, the settings vary in accordance with the job in hand. For example, most printer drivers (the software which 'drives' the printer) allow you to specify whether or not you want pictures printed. Additionally, they often allow you to specify the resolution or print quality of the output...

Selecting the printer and/or settings

Just before you're ready to print a document, pull down the File menu and click Print. Now do the following:

Click here; select the printer you want from the list

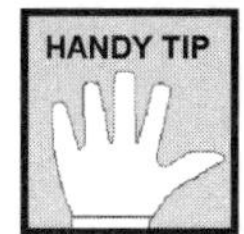

Set any print options which are required *before* carrying out step 3 (see 'Customised Printing' later for how to do this).

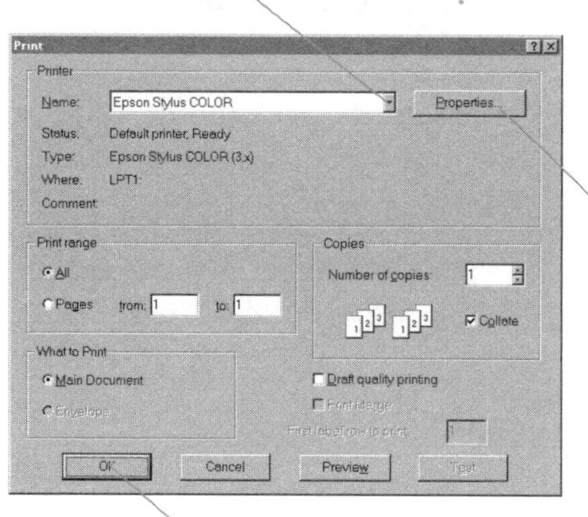

2 Click here to adjust the printer settings (for how to do this, see your printer's manual)

3 Click here to begin printing

Printing - an overview

Once the active document is how you want it (and you've customised the printer setup appropriately), the next stage is to print it out. The Word Processor makes this process easy and straightforward. It lets you set a variety of options before you do so.

Alternatively, you can simply opt to print your document with the default options in force (the Word Processor provides a 'fast track' approach to this).

Available print options include:

- the number of copies you want printed

- whether you want the copies 'collated'. This is the process whereby Works prints one full copy at a time. For instance, if you're printing three copies of a 40-page document, Works prints pages 1-40 of the first document, followed by pages 1-40 of the second and pages 1-40 of the third.

- which pages you want printed

- the quality of the eventual output. With many printers, the Word Processor module allows you to print in Draft (with minimal formatting) for proofing purposes. This means that:

  - font styles (bold, italic, underline and strikethrough), pictures and colours don't print.

  - Works uses your default printer font (very often Courier or a variation on this) instead of the font you allocated.

  This option generally ensures that documents print more rapidly.

You can 'mix and match' these, as appropriate.

Printing - the fast track approach

Since documents and printing needs vary dramatically, it's often necessary to customise print options before you begin printing.

For example, if you've created a document which contains numerous pictures, you may well want to print out a draft copy for proofing purposes prior to printing the definitive version (although Print Preview mode provides a very effective indication of how a document will look when printed, there are still errors which are only detectable when you're working with hard copy). In this situation, you may wish to print in Draft mode (with minimal formatting).

For how to set your own print options, see the 'Customised printing' topic.

On the other hand, simple documents can often benefit from a simple approach. In this case, you may well be content to print using the default options. Works recognises this and provides a method which bypasses the standard Print dialog, and is therefore much quicker and easier to use.

Printing with the current print options

First, ensure your printer is ready, and your document is ready to print. Make sure the toolbar is visible. (If it isn't, pull down the View menu and click Toolbar).

Now do the following:

Works starts printing the active document immediately.

Customised printing

If you need to set revised print options before printing, pull down the File menu and click Print. Now carry out steps 1-4 below, as appropriate. To inspect your document in Print Preview mode before printing, follow steps 5 and 6. Finally, carry out step 7.

You can use a keyboard shortcut to produce the Print dialog: simply press Ctrl+P.

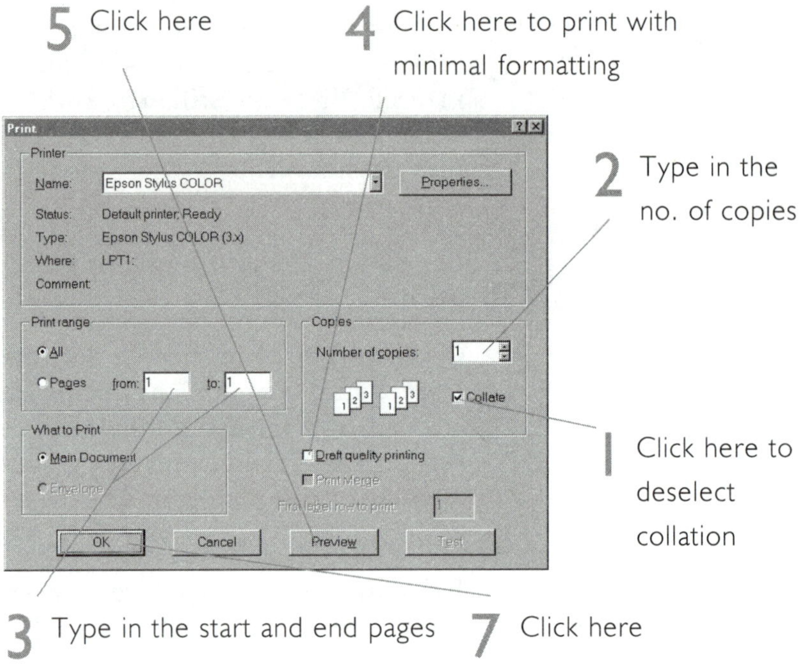

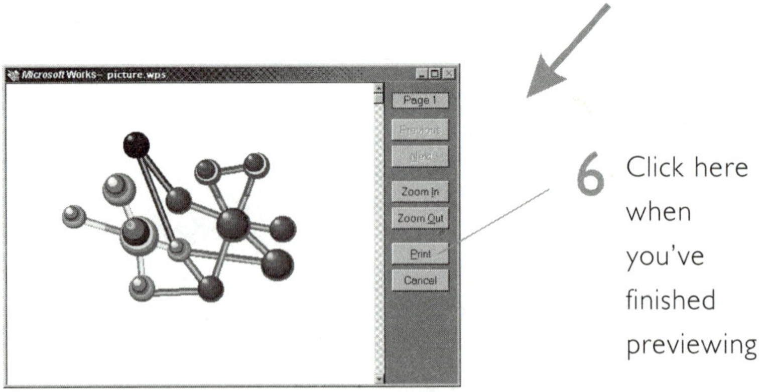

5 Click here

4 Click here to print with minimal formatting

2 Type in the no. of copies

| Click here to deselect collation

3 Type in the start and end pages

7 Click here

6 Click here when you've finished previewing

After step 7, Works starts printing the active document.

The Spreadsheet

This chapter gives you the fundamentals of using the Spreadsheet module. You'll learn how to work with data and formulas, and how to move around through spreadsheets. You'll also learn how to locate data, and make it more visually effective. Finally, you'll customise page layout/printing.

Covers

The Spreadsheet screen

Below is a detailed illustration of the Spreadsheet screen.

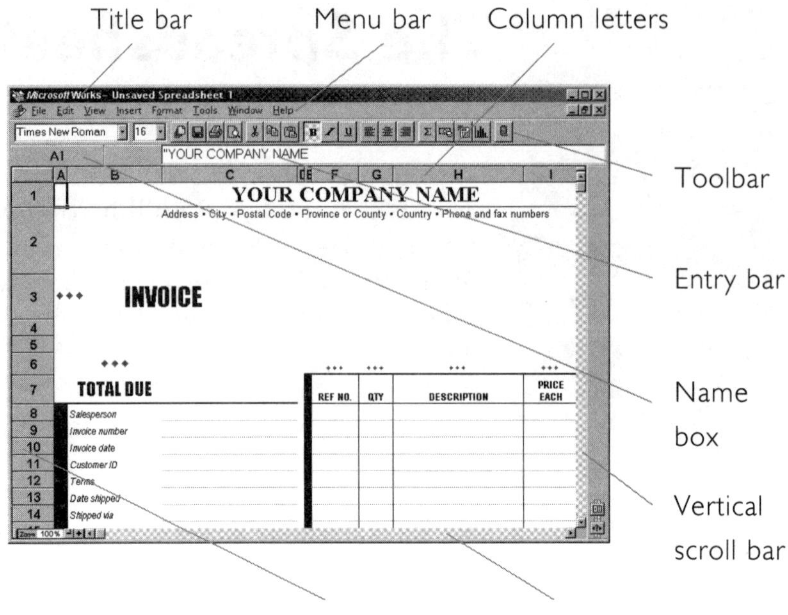

This is the Zoom area. The screen components here are used to adjust magnification levels. See the 'Changing Zoom levels' topic later.

Some of these – e.g. the scroll bars – are standard to just about all programs which run under Windows. One – the toolbar – can be hidden, if required.

Specifying whether the toolbar displays

Pull down the View menu. Then do the following:

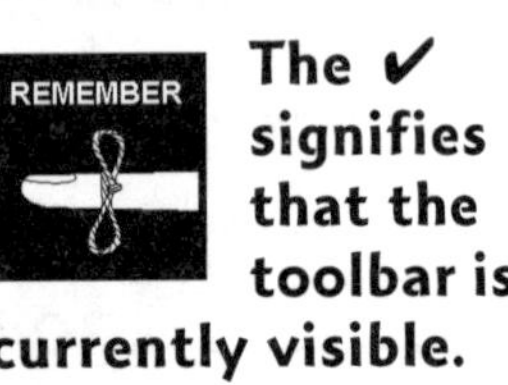

The ✔ signifies that the toolbar is currently visible.

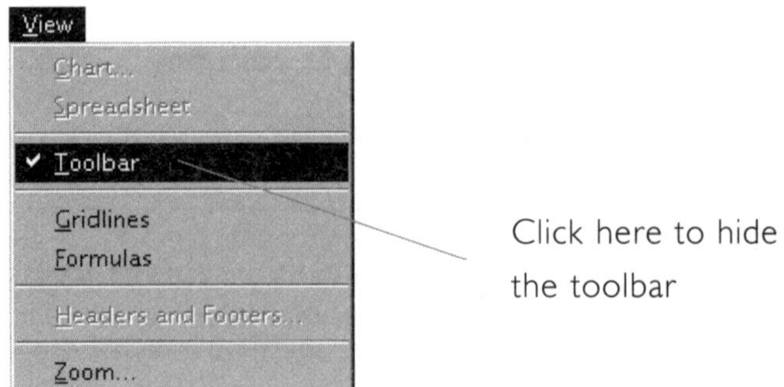

Click here to hide the toolbar

Entering data (1)

When you start the Works Spreadsheet module, you can use the Task Launcher to create a new blank spreadsheet (see Section 1 for how to do this). The result will look something like this:

Works applies the following names to new blank spreadsheets: 'Spreadsheet 1', 'Spreadsheet 2' etc.

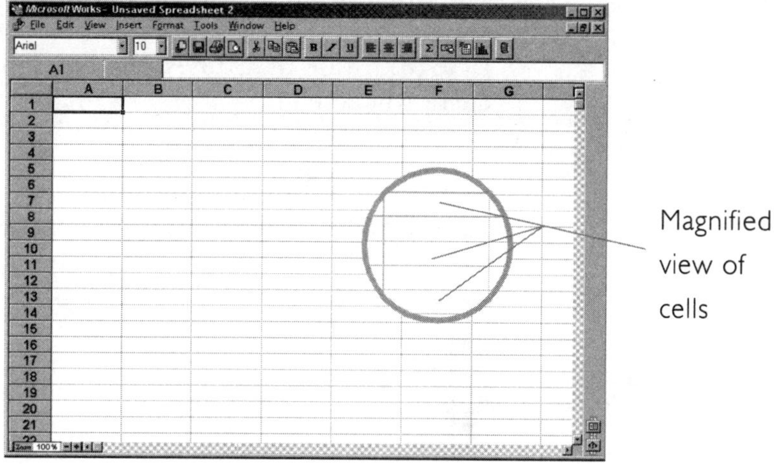

Magnified view of cells

This means that you can start entering data immediately.

In the Spreadsheet module, you can enter the following basic data types:

Columns are vertical, rows horizontal. Each spreadsheet can have as many as 256 columns and 16,384 rows, making a grand total of 4,194,304 cells.

*   values (i.e. numbers)

*   text (e.g. headings and explanatory material)

*   functions (e.g. Sine or Cosine)

*   formulas (combinations of values, text and functions)

You enter data into 'cells'. Cells are formed where rows and columns intersect. In the most basic sense, collections of rows/columns and cells are known as spreadsheets.

Entering data (2)

Although you can enter data *directly* into a cell (by simply clicking in it and typing it in), there's another method you can use which is often easier. The Spreadsheet provides a special screen component known as the Entry bar.

The illustration below shows the end of a blank spreadsheet. Some sample text has been inserted into cell IV16384 (note that the Name box tells you which cell is currently active).

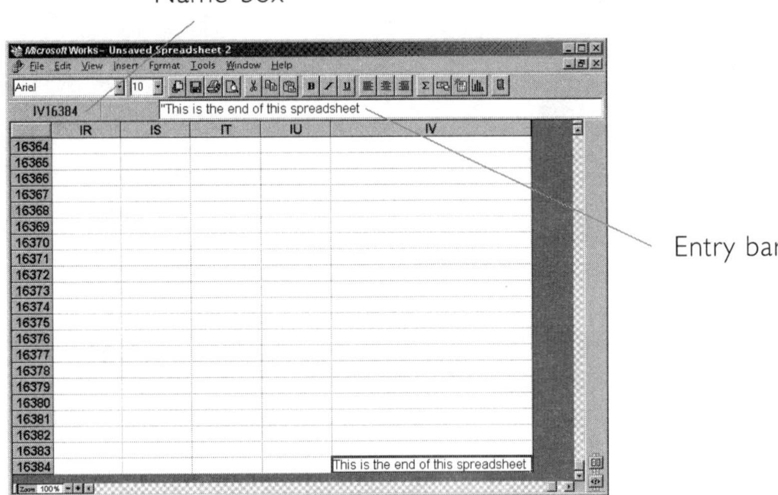

Entering data via the Entry bar

Click the cell you want to insert data into. Then click the Entry bar. Type in the data. Then follow step 1 below. If you decide not to proceed with the operation, follow step 2 instead:

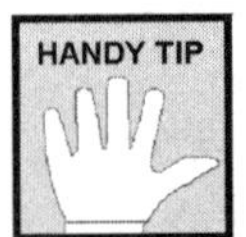

You can use a keyboard route to confirm operations in the Entry bar: simply press Return.

1 Click here

2 Click here to cancel the operation

Modifying existing data

You can amend the contents of a cell in two ways:

- via the Entry bar

- from within the cell

When you use either of these methods, the Spreadsheet enters a special state known as Edit Mode.

Amending existing data using the Entry bar

Click the cell whose contents you want to change. Then click in the Entry bar. Make the appropriate revisions and/or additions. Then press Return. The relevant cell is updated.

Amending existing data internally

Click the cell whose contents you want to change. Press F2. Make the appropriate revisions and/or additions *within the cell.* Then press Return.

The illustration below shows a section of a spreadsheet created with the INVOICE TaskWizard.

A magnified view of cell D12, in Edit Mode

Working with cell ranges

When you're working with more than one cell, it's often convenient and useful to organise them in 'ranges'.

To make the underlying structure of a spreadsheet's component cells more visible, pull down the View menu and click Gridlines. Repeat this procedure if you need to hide the structure.

A range is a rectangular arrangement of cells. In the illustration below, cells B11, C11, D11, E11, F11, G11, B12, C12, D12, E12, F12 and G12 have been selected.

A selected cell range

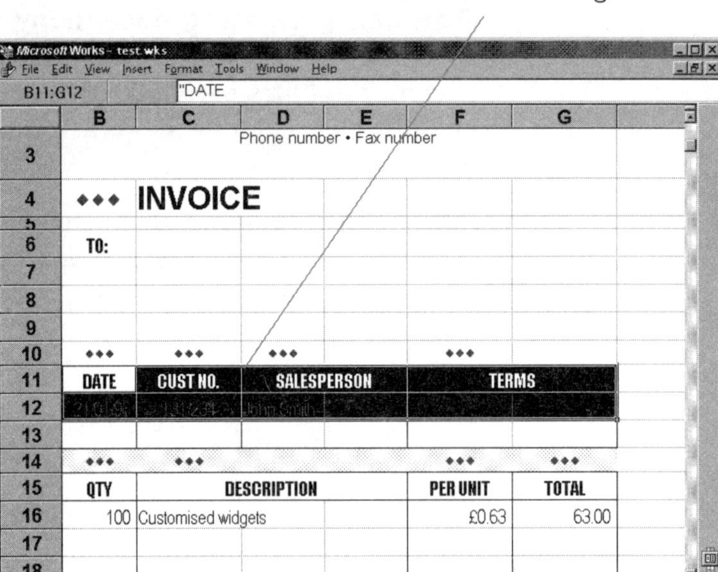

Cells in a selected range are coloured black, with the exception of the first.

Cell 'shorthand'

The above description of the relevant cells is very cumbersome. It's much more useful to use a form of shorthand. The Spreadsheet module (using the start and end cells as reference points) refers to these cells as:

B11:G12

This notation system makes it much easier to refer to sizeable cell ranges.

Moving around in spreadsheets (1)

Spreadsheets can be huge. Moving to cells which happen currently to be visible is easy: you simply click in the relevant cell. However, the Spreadsheet module provides several techniques you can use to jump to less accessible areas.

Using the scroll bars

Use any of the following methods:

1. To scroll quickly to another section of the active spreadsheet, drag the scroll box along the scroll bar until you reach it.

2. To move one window to the left or right, click to the left or right of the scroll box in the horizontal scroll bar.

3. To move one window up or down, click above or below the scroll box in the vertical scroll bar.

4. To move up or down by one row, click the arrows in the vertical scroll bar.

5. To move left or right by one column, click the arrows in the horizontal scroll bar.

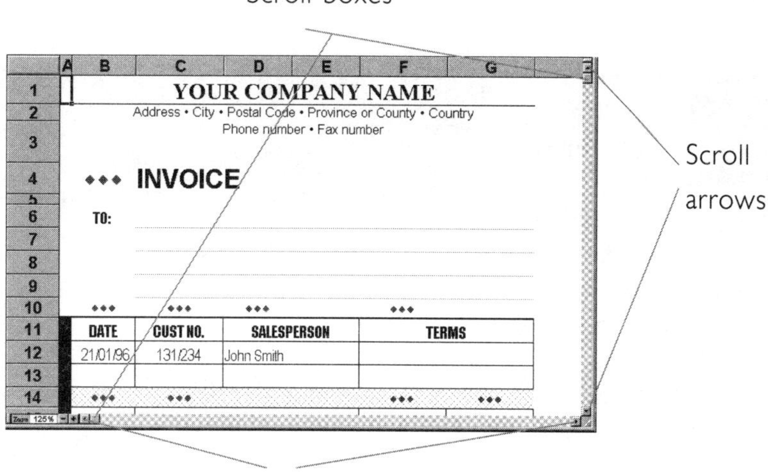

Moving around in spreadsheets (2)

Using the keyboard

You can use the following techniques:

1. Use the cursor keys to move one cell left, right, up or down.

2. Hold down Ctrl as you use 1 above; this jumps to the edge of the current section (e.g. if cell B11 is active and you hold down Ctrl as you press →, Works jumps to IV11, the last cell in row 11).

3. Press Home to jump to the first cell in the active row, or Ctrl+Home to move to A1.

4. Press Page Up or Page Down to move up or down by one screen.

5. Press Ctrl+Page Down to move one screen to the right, or Ctrl+Page Up to move one screen to the left.

Using the Go To dialog

The Spreadsheet provides a special dialog which you can use to specify precise cell destinations.

Pull down the Edit menu and click Go To. Now do the following:

You can use a keyboard shortcut to launch the Go To dialog: simply press F5, or Ctrl+G.

Re step 1 - a cell's 'reference' (or 'address') identifies it in relation to its position in a spreadsheet, e.g. B11 or H23. You can also type in cell ranges here (e.g. B11:C15).

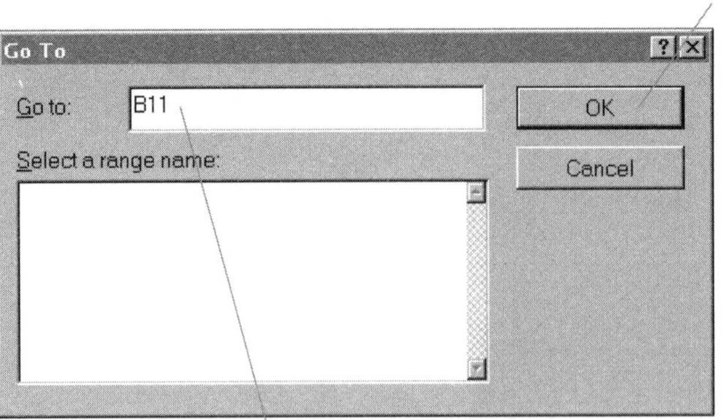

Changing Zoom levels (1)

The ability to vary the level of magnification for the active document is especially useful for spreadsheets, which very often occupy more space than can be accommodated on-screen at any given time. Sometimes, it's helpful to 'zoom out' (i.e. decrease the magnification) so that you can take an overview; at other times, you'll need to 'zoom in' (increase the magnification) to work in greater detail.

You can alter magnification levels in the Spreadsheet module:

- with the use of the Zoom area

- with the Zoom dialog

Using the Zoom area

You can use the Zoom area (at the base of the screen) to alter zoom levels with the minimum of effort. Carry out step 1 or 2, or steps 3&4, as appropriate:

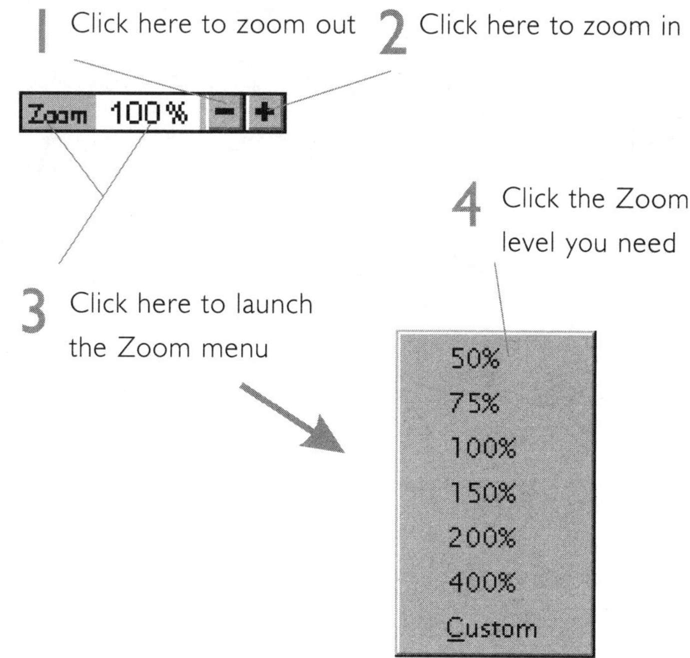

Re step 4 - clicking Custom produces the Zoom dialog. See the 'Changing Zoom levels (2)' topic for how to use this.

Changing Zoom levels (2)

Using the Zoom dialog

Using the Zoom dialog, you can perform either of the following:

- choose from preset zoom levels (e.g. 200%, 100%, 75%)

- specify your own zoom percentage

If you want to impose your own, custom zoom level, it's probably easier, quicker and more convenient to use the Zoom dialog.

Pull down the View menu and click Zoom. Now carry out step 1 or 2 below. Finally, follow step 3.

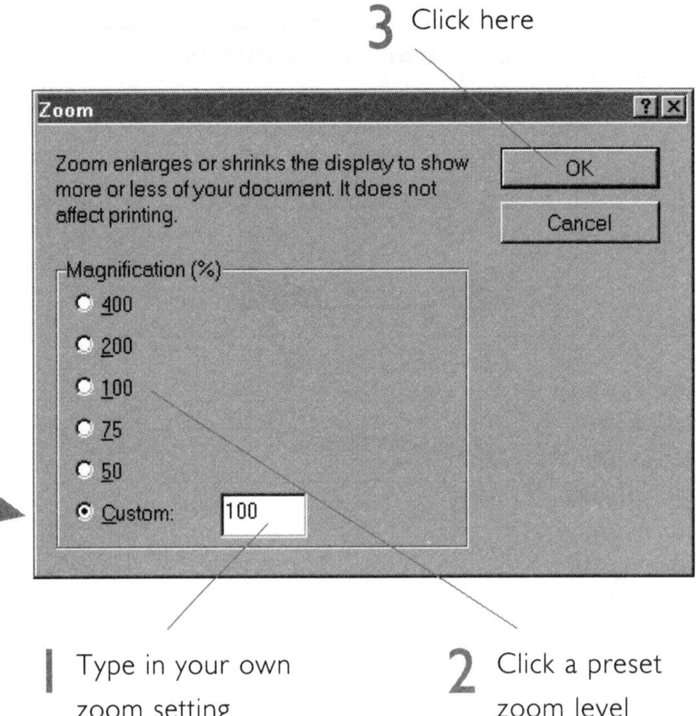

Entries here must lie in the range 25%-1000%.

1 Type in your own zoom setting

2 Click a preset zoom level

Selection techniques (1)

Before you can carry out any editing operations on cells in the Spreadsheet module, you have to select them first. Selecting a single cell is very easy: you merely click in it. However, there are a variety of selection techniques which you can use to select more than one cell simultaneously.

Selecting cell ranges with the mouse

The easiest way to select more than one cell at a time is to use the mouse.

Click in the first cell in the range; hold down the left mouse button and drag over the remaining cells. Release the mouse button.

Selecting cell ranges with the keyboard

There are two separate techniques you can use:

With the exception of the first cell, a selected range is filled with black.

- Position the cell pointer over the first cell in the range. Hold down one Shift key as you use the relevant cursor key to extend the selection. Release the keys when the correct selection has been defined.

- Position the cell pointer over the first cell in the range. Press F8 to enter Selection mode. Use the cursor keys to define the selection area (see the illustration below). Finally, press F8 again to leave Selection mode.

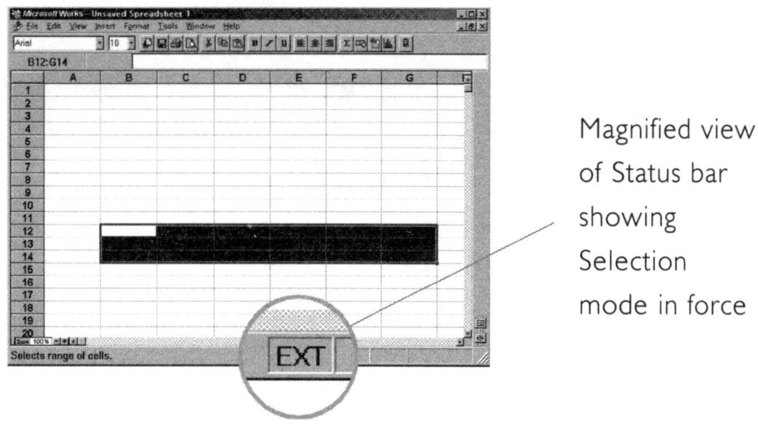

Magnified view of Status bar showing Selection mode in force

Selection techniques (2)

Selecting a single row or column

To select every cell within a row or column automatically, click on the row or column heading.

Column heading

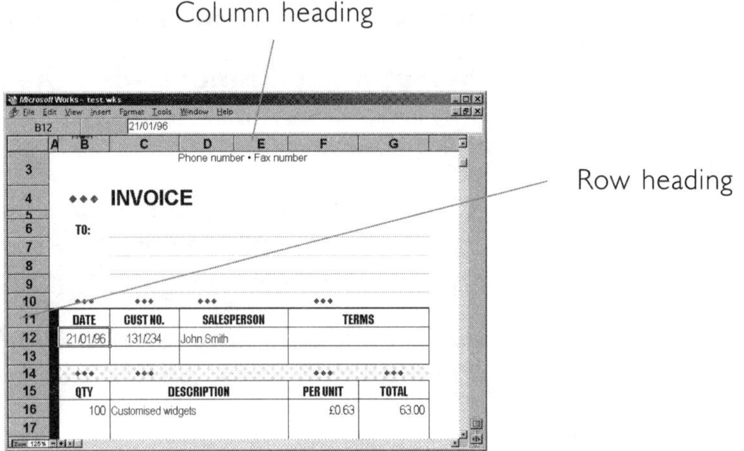

Row heading

Selecting multiple rows or columns

To select more than one row or column, click on the row or column heading. Hold down the left mouse button and drag to select adjacent rows or columns.

Selecting an entire spreadsheet

Click the Select All button:

A magnified view of the Select All button

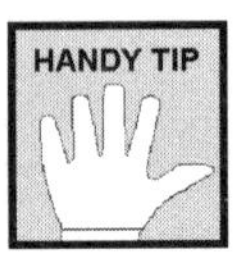

You can use a keyboard shortcut to select every cell automatically: simply press Ctrl+A, or Ctrl+Shift+F8.

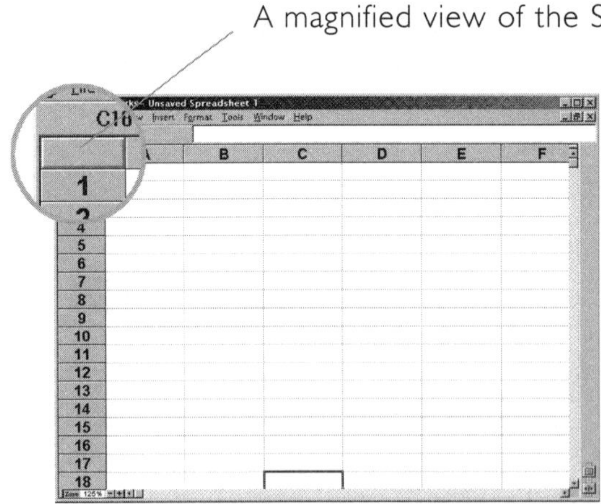

Formulas - an overview

Formulas are cell entries which define how other values relate to each other.

As a very simple example, consider the following:

This is part of the spreadsheet created with the INVOICE TaskWizard. Cell G16 has been defined so that it multiplies the contents of cells B16 and F16. Obviously, in this instance you could insert the result easily enough yourself because the values are so small, and because we're only dealing with a small number of cells. But what happens if the cell values are larger and/or more numerous, or – more to the point – if they're liable to change frequently?

The answer is to insert a formula which carries out the necessary calculation automatically.

If you look at the Entry bar in the illustration, you'll see the formula which does this:

=IF(F16,F16*B16,"")

This is a fairly complex formula. Basically, it instructs Works to inspect cell F16. If an entry is found, the contents should be multiplied by the contents of B16, and the results displayed.

> **HANDY TIP**
>
> **The 'F16*B16' component tells Works to multiply the contents of the two cells. The 'IF' before the bracket is the conditional operator.**

Inserting a formula

Arguments (e.g. cell references) relating to functions are always contained in brackets.

All formulas in the Spreadsheet begin with an equals sign. This is usually followed by a permutation of the following:

- an operand (cell reference, e.g. B4)

- a function (e.g. the summation function, SUM)

- an arithmetical operator (+, –, /, * and ^)

- comparison operators (=, <, >, <=, >= and <>)

The Spreadsheet supports a very wide range of functions organised into numerous categories. For more information on how to insert functions, see the 'Functions – an overview' topic.

The mathematical operators are (in the order in which they appear in the bulleted list): *plus, minus, divide, multiply* and *exponential*.

The comparison operators are (in the order in which they appear in the list): *equals, less than, greater than, less than or equal to, greater than or equal to* and *not equal to*.

There are two ways to enter formulas:

Entering a formula directly into the cell

Click the cell in which you want to insert a formula. Then type =, followed by your formula. When you've finished, press Return.

Entering a formula into the Entry bar

This is usually the most convenient method.

Click the cell in which you want to insert a formula. Then click in the Entry bar. Type =, followed by your formula. When you've finished, press Return or do the following:

Click here

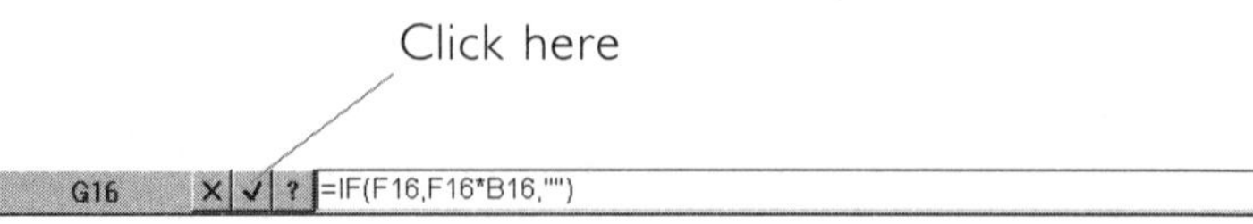

Functions - an overview

Functions are pre-defined, built-in tools which accomplish specific tasks and then display the result. These tasks are very often calculations; occasionally, however, they're considerably more generalised (e.g. some functions simply return dates and/or times). In effect, functions replace one or more formulas.

The Spreadsheet module organises its functions under the following headings:

- Financial

- Date and Time

- Math and Trig

- Statistical

- Lookup and Ref

- Text

- Logical

- Informational

Works provides a special shortcut (called Easy Calc) which makes entering functions much easier and more straightforward. Easy Calc is very useful for the following reasons:

- It provides access to a large number of functions from a centralised source.

- It ensures that functions are entered with the correct syntax.

Functions can only be used in formulas. Note, however, that the result displays in the host cell, rather than the underlying function/formula.

You can, however, have Works display formulas/ functions in situ within the spreadsheet. Simply pull down the View menu and click Formulas.

Using Easy Calc

If you follow step 2, Works launches the Insert Function dialog. Pick a function category in the Category field, then select the relevant function in the Choose a function box. Click Insert. Now follow the instructions in the two remaining Easy Calc dialogs below.

Inserting a function with Easy Calc

At the relevant juncture during the process of inserting a formula, pull down the Tools menu and click Easy Calc. Now carry out step 1 OR 2 below:

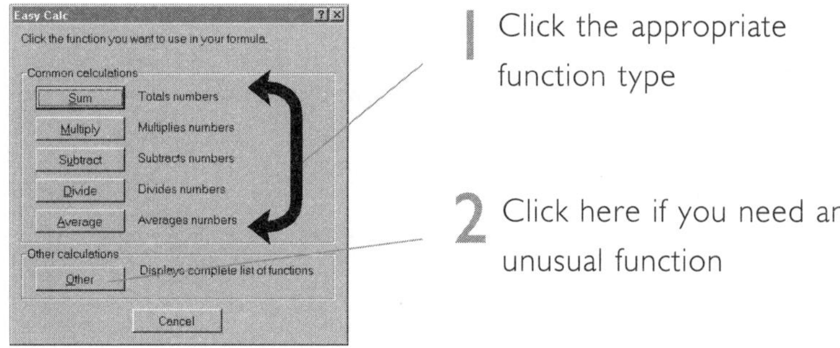

1 Click the appropriate function type

2 Click here if you need an unusual function

Now complete the following dialogs (the contents vary with the function selected):

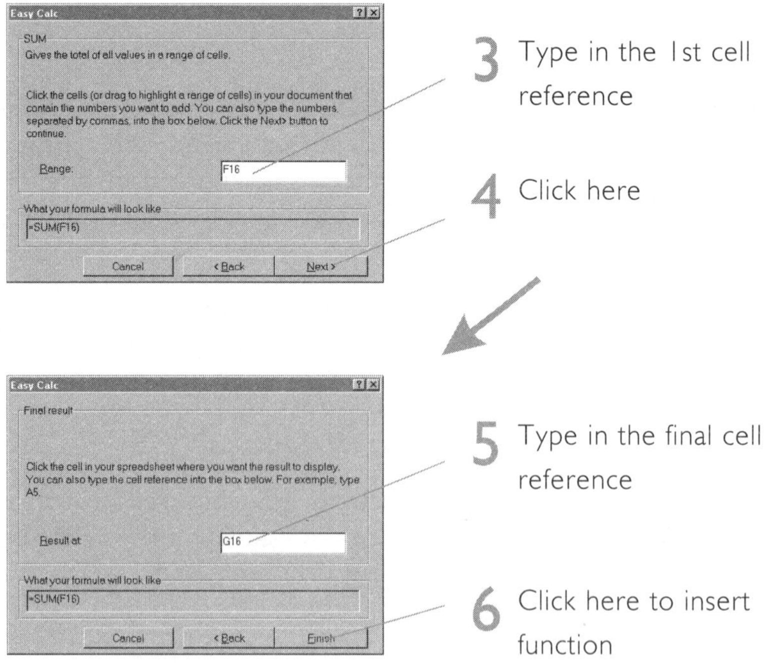

3 Type in the 1st cell reference

4 Click here

5 Type in the final cell reference

6 Click here to insert function

Amending row/column sizes

Sooner or later, you'll find it necessary to change the dimensions of rows or columns. This necessity arises when there is too much data in cells to display adequately. You can enlarge or shrink single or multiple rows/columns.

Changing row height

To change one row's height, click the row heading. If you want to change multiple rows, hold down Shift and click the appropriate extra headings. Then pull down the Format menu and click Row Height. Carry out the following steps:

2 Click here

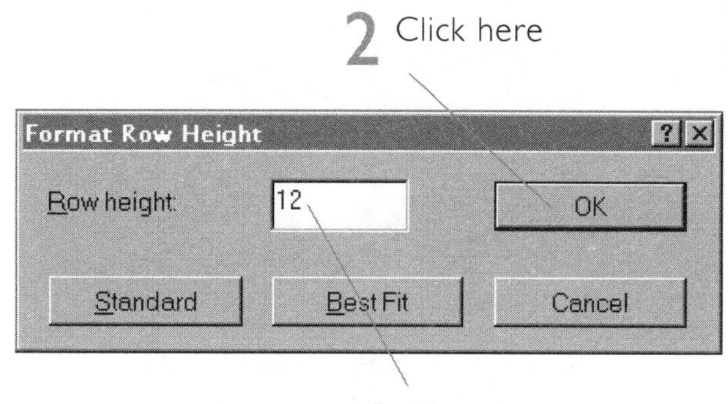

Type in the new height

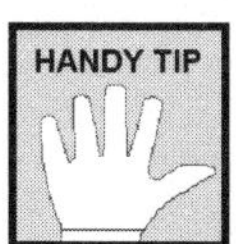

Works has a useful 'best fit' feature. Simply click Best Fit in either dialog to have the row(s) or column(s) adjust themselves automatically to their contents.

Changing column widths

To change one column's width, click the column heading. If you want to change multiple columns, hold down Shift and click the appropriate extra headings. Then pull down the Format menu and click Column Width. Now do the following:

2 Click here

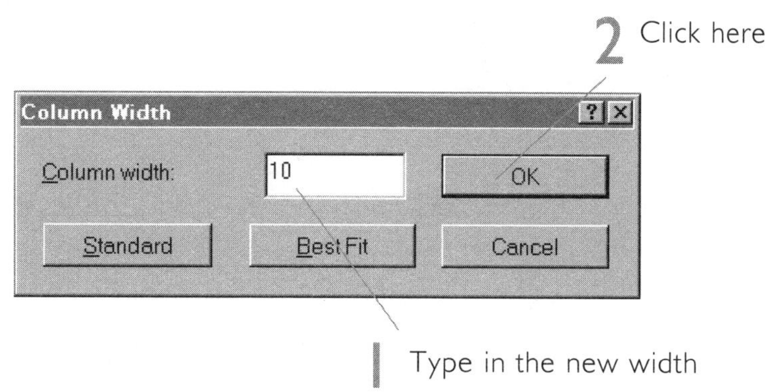

Type in the new width

Inserting rows or columns

You can insert additional rows or columns into spreadsheets.

Inserting a new row or column

First, select one or more cells within the row(s) or column(s) where you want to carry out the insert operation. Now pull down the Insert menu and carry out step 1 or 2 below:

If you select cells in more than one row or column, Works inserts the equivalent number of new rows or columns.

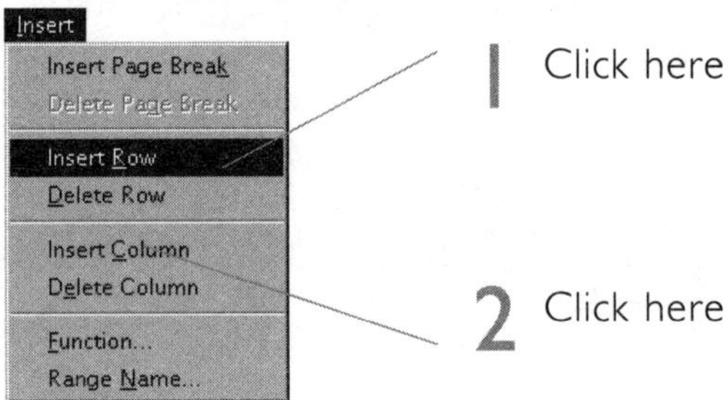

1 Click here

2 Click here

The new row(s) or column(s) are inserted immediately.

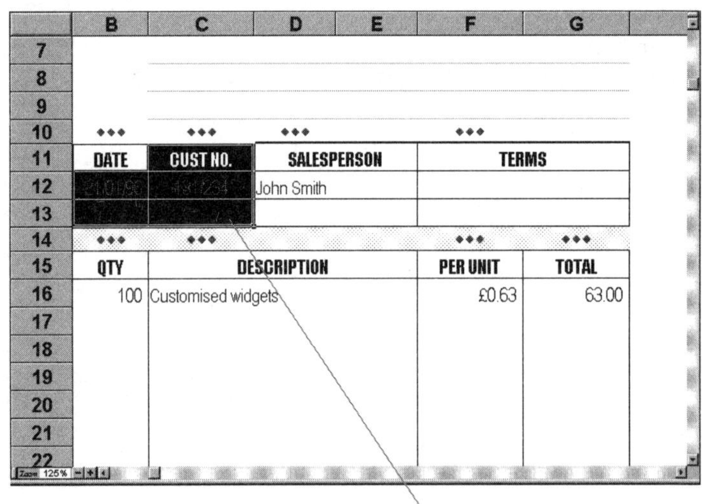

Here, two new columns or three new rows are being added

Working with fills

The Spreadsheet module lets you duplicate the contents of a selected cell down a column or across a row easily and conveniently.

Use this technique to save time and effort.

Duplicating a cell

Click the cell whose contents you want to duplicate. Then move the mouse pointer over the appropriate border. Click and hold down the button; drag the border over the cells into which you want the contents inserted. Release the button.

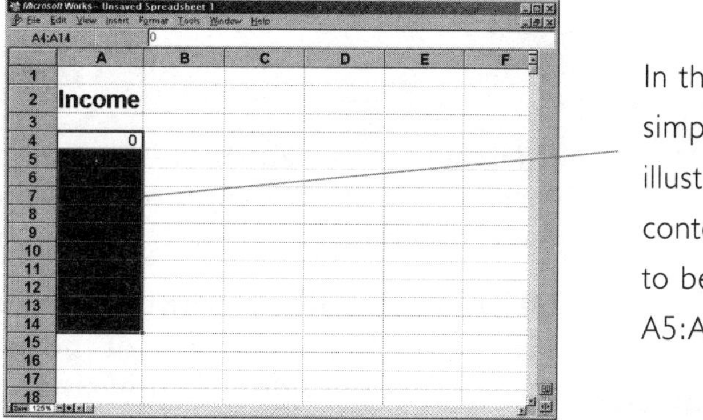

In this (admittedly simplistic) illustration, the contents of A4 are to be copied into A5:A14.

Now pull down the Edit menu and click Fill Right or Fill Down, as appropriate.

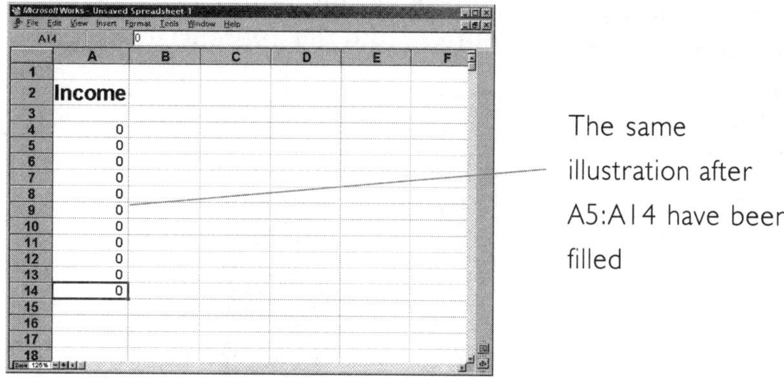

The same illustration after A5:A14 have been filled

Using AutoFill

You can also carry out fills which *extrapolate* cell contents over the specified cells – Works calls these 'data series'. Look at the next illustration:

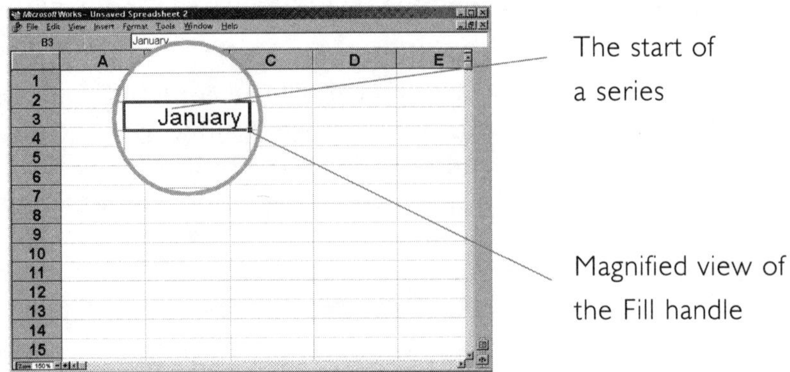

If (as here) you wanted to insert month names in successive cells in a column, you could do so manually. But there's a much easier way. You can use AutoFill.

Using AutoFill to create a series

Type in the first element(s) of the series in consecutive cells. Select the cells. Then position the mouse pointer over the Fill handle in the bottom right-hand corner of the last cell (the pointer changes to a cross-hair). Hold down the left mouse button and drag the handle over the cells into which you want to extend the series. When you release the mouse button, Works extrapolates the initial entry or entries into the appropriate series.

REMEMBER

In addition to months, data series can consist of numbers (e.g. 1, 2, 3, 4 etc.); days of the week; years; and alphanumeric combinations (e.g. Week 1, Week 2, Week 3 etc.).

Microsoft Works in easy steps

Changing number formats

The Spreadsheet module lets you apply various formatting enhancements to cells and their contents. You can:

• specify a number format

• customise the font, type size and style of contents

• specify cell alignment

• border and/or shade cells

Specifying a number format

You can customise the way cell contents (e.g. numbers and dates/times) display. For example, you can specify at what point numbers are rounded up. Available formats are organised under several general categories. These include: Date, Percent and Fraction.

Select the cells whose contents you want to customise. Pull down the Format menu and click Number. Now do the following:

Ensure the Number tab is active

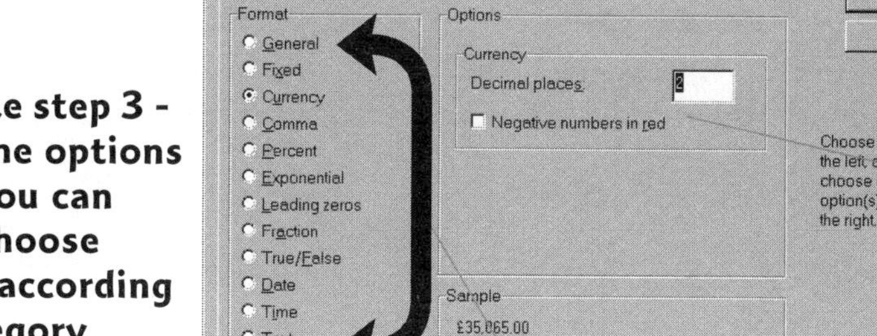

4 Click here

3 Complete the relevant options

2 Click the applicable category

REMEMBER **Re step 3 – the options you can choose from vary according to the category chosen. Complete them as necessary.**

Changing fonts and styles

The Spreadsheet module lets you carry out the following actions on cell contents (numbers, text or combinations of both):

- apply a new font

- apply a new type size

- apply a font style (*Italic*, **Bold**, <u>Underlining</u> or ~~Strikethrough~~)

- apply a colour

Amending the appearance of cell contents

Select the cell(s) whose contents you want to reformat. Pull down the Format menu and click Font and Style. Carry out step 1 below. Now follow any of steps 2-5, as appropriate. Finally, carry out step 6.

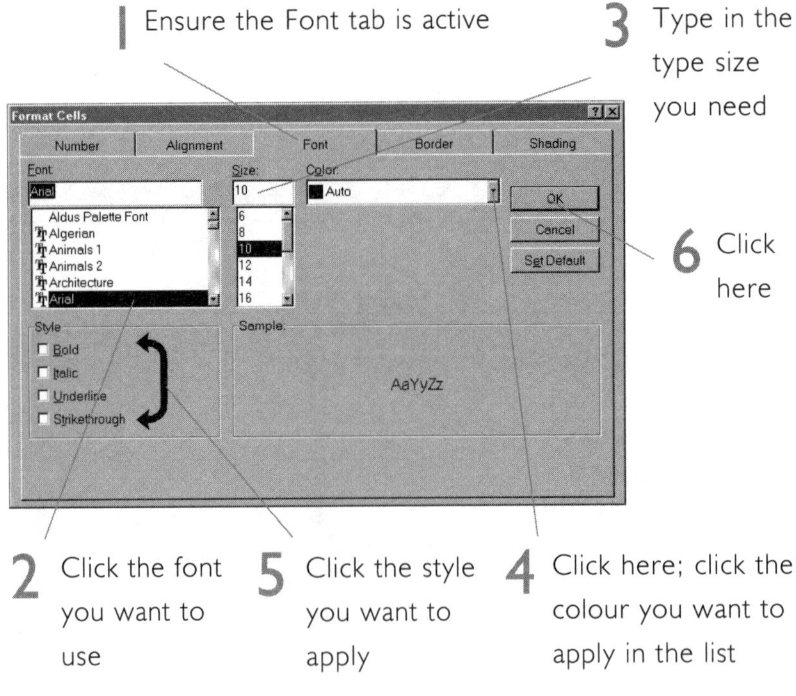

Cell alignment (1)

By default, Works aligns text to the left of cells, and numbers to the right. However, if you want you can change this.

You can specify alignment under two broad headings: Horizontal and Vertical.

Horizontal alignment

The main options are:

General	the default (see above)
Left	contents are aligned from the left
Right	contents are aligned from the right
Center	contents are centred
Fill	contents are duplicated so that they fill the cell
Center across selection	contents are centred across more than one cell (if you pre-selected a cell range)

Vertical alignment

Available options are:

Top	cell contents align with the top of the cell(s)
Center	contents are centred
Bottom	contents align with the cell bottom

Most of these settings parallel features found in the Word Processor module (and in many other word processors). The difference, however, lies in the fact that in spreadsheets Works has to align data within the bounds of cells rather than a page. When it aligns text, it often needs to employ its own version of text wrap. See 'Cell alignment (2)' for more information on this.

Cell alignment (2)

By default, when text is too large for the host cell, Works overflows the surplus into adjacent cells to the right. However, you can opt to have the Spreadsheet module force the text onto separate lines within the original cell. This process is called text wrap.

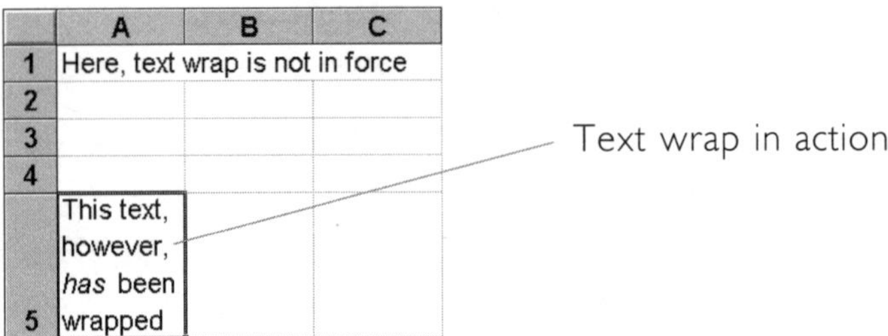

Text wrap in action

Customising cell alignment & applying text wrap

Select the relevant cell(s). Pull down the Format menu and click Alignment. Carry out step 1 below. Now follow any or all of steps 2-4, as appropriate. Finally, carry out step 5.

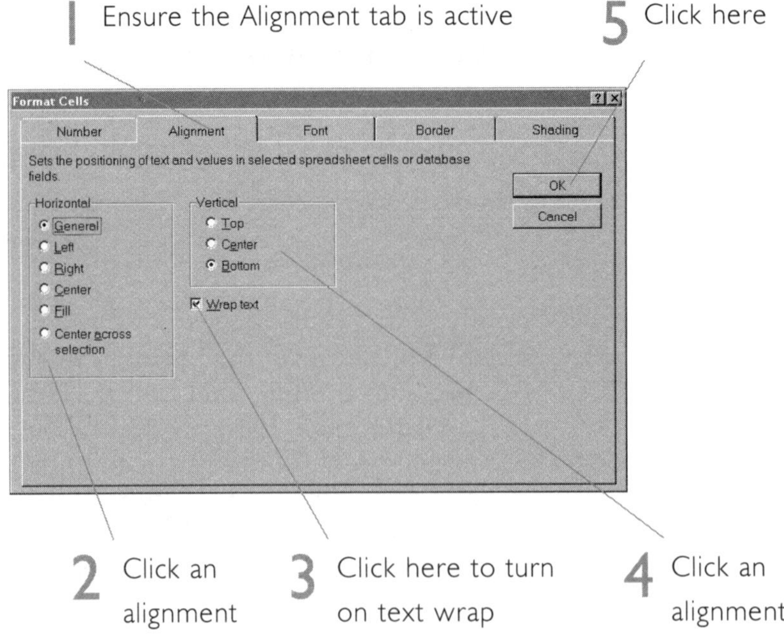

Bordering cells

Works lets you define a border around:

- the perimeter of a selected cell range

- the individual cells within a selected cell range

- specific sides within a cell range

You can customise the border by choosing from a selection of pre-defined border styles. You can also colour the border, if required.

Applying a cell border

First, select the cell range you want to border. Pull down the Format menu and click Border. Now carry out steps 1 and 2 below. Step 3 is optional. Finally, follow steps 4 and 5. If you're setting multiple border options, repeat steps 2-4 as required.

Re step 4 – Outline borders the perimeter of the selected cells. The other options (you can click more than 1) affect *individual* sides.

1 Ensure the Border tab is active

2 Click the relevant line style option

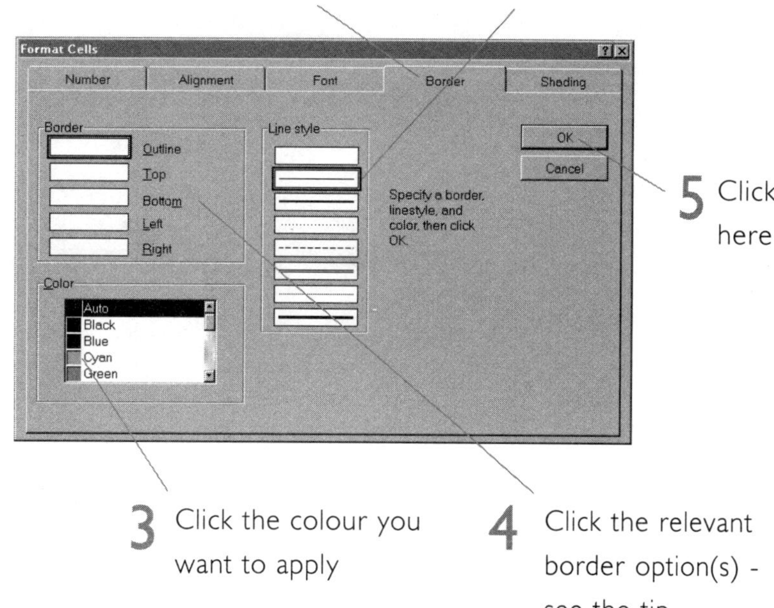

5 Click here

3 Click the colour you want to apply

4 Click the relevant border option(s) - see the tip

Shading cells

Works lets you apply the following to cells:

- a pattern

- a pattern colour

- a background colour

You can do any of these singly, or in combination. Interesting effects can be achieved by using pattern colours with coloured backgrounds.

Applying a pattern or background

First, select the cell range you want to shade. Pull down the Format menu and click Shading. Now carry out step 1 below. Follow steps 2, 3 or 4 as appropriate. Finally, carry out step 5:

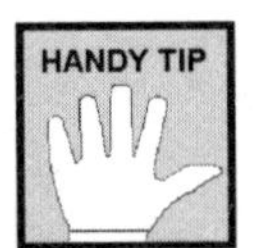

The Sample area previews how your background and pattern/colour will look.

1 Ensure the Shading tab is active

5 Click here

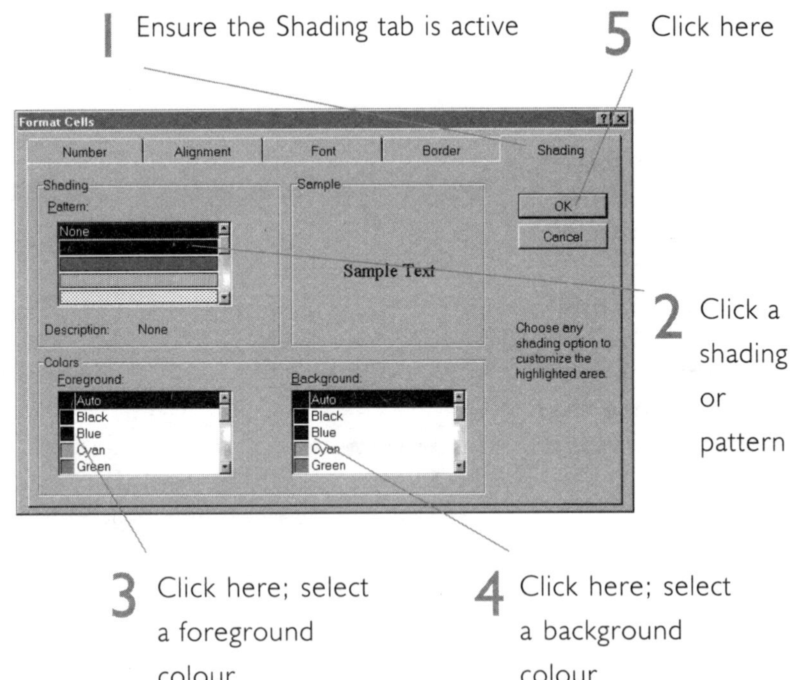

2 Click a shading or pattern

3 Click here; select a foreground colour

4 Click here; select a background colour

AutoFormat

Works provides a shortcut to the formatting of spreadsheet data: AutoFormat.

AutoFormat consists of 16 pre-defined formatting schemes. These incorporate specific excerpts from the font, number, alignment, border and shading options discussed earlier. You can apply any of these schemes (and their associated formatting) to selected cell ranges with just a few mouse clicks. Doing this saves a lot of time and effort, and the results are dependably professional.

AutoFormat works with most arrangements of spreadsheet data. However, if the effect you achieve isn't what you want, you can 'undo' it (providing you've carried out no intervening editing operations) by pressing Ctrl+Z.

Using AutoFormat

First, select the cell range you want to apply an automatic format to. Pull down the Format menu and click AutoFormat. Now carry out steps 1 and 2 below:

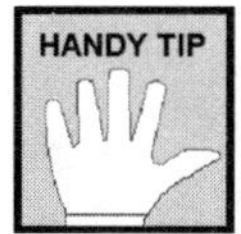

The Example field previews how your data will look with the specified AutoFormat.

2 Click here

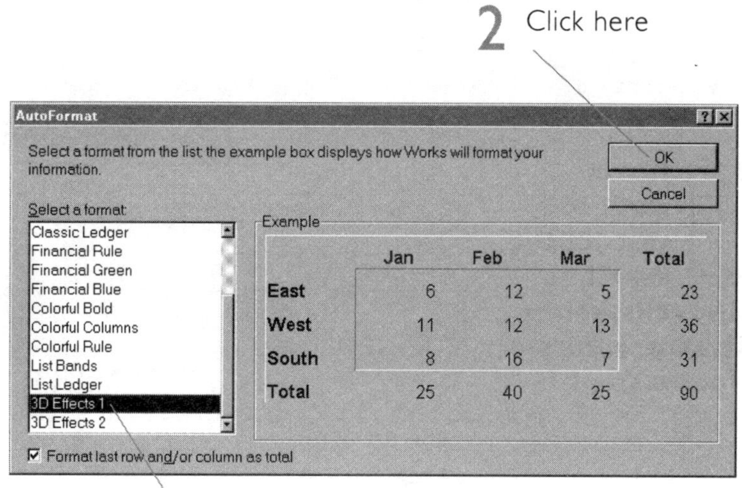

Click the format you
want to apply

Find operations

The Spreadsheet lets you search for and jump to text and/ or numbers (in short, any information) in your spreadsheets. This is a particularly useful feature when spreadsheets become large and complex, as they almost invariably do.

In Find operations, you can specify whether Works searches:

- by columns or rows

- in cells which contain formulas

- in cells which don't contain formulas

Searching for data

Place the mouse pointer at the location in the active spreadsheet from which you want the search to begin. Pull down the Edit menu and click Find. (Or press Ctrl+F). Now carry out step 1 below, then any of steps 2-3. Finally, carry out step 4.

1 Type in the data you want to find

4 Click here

If you want to restrict the search to specific cells, select a cell range *before* you follow steps 1-4.

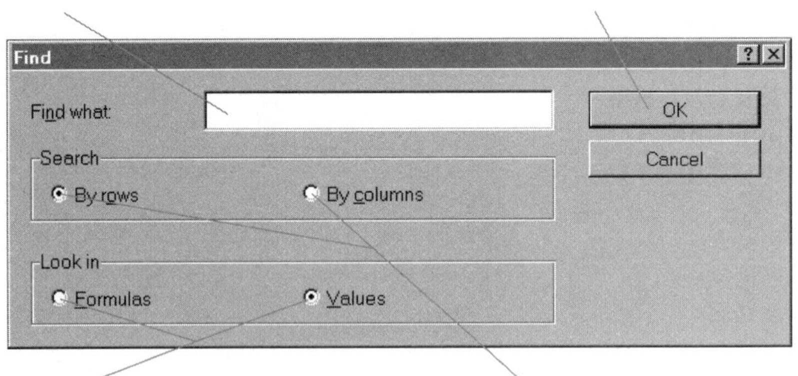

2 To limit the search, click the relevant option

3 To specify the search direction, click the relevant option

Search-and-replace operations

When you search for data, you can also – if you want – have Works replace it with something else.

Search-and-replace operations can be organised by rows or by columns. However, unlike straight searches, you can't specify whether Works looks in cells which contain formulas or those which don't.

Running a search-and-replace operation

Place the mouse pointer at the location in the active spreadsheet from which you want the search to begin. Pull down the Edit menu and click Replace. Now carry out step 1 below, then any of steps 2-3. Now do *one* of the following:

- Follow step 4. When Works locates the first search target, carry out step 5 to have it replaced. Repeat this process as often as necessary.

- Carry out step 6 to have Works find every target and replace it automatically.

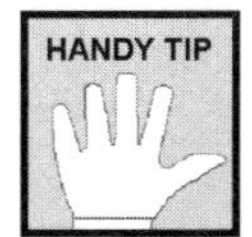

If you want to restrict the search-and-replace operation to specific cells, select a cell range *before* you follow the procedures outlined here.

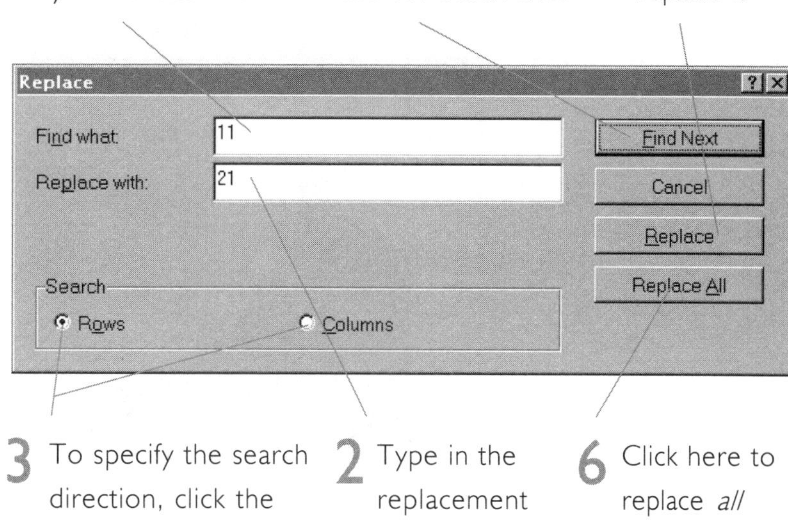

Charting - an overview

The Spreadsheet module has comprehensive charting capabilities. You can have it convert selected data into its visual equivalent. To do this, Works offers 12 chart formats:

- Area
- Bar
- Line
- Pie
- Stacked Line
- X-Y (Scatter)

- Radar
- Combination
- 3-D Area
- 3-D Bar
- 3-D Line
- 3-D Pie

When you create a chart, Works launches it in a separate Chart Editor window. You can have as many as 8 charts associated with any spreadsheet.

Works uses a special dialog to make the process of creating charts as easy and convenient as possible.

The illustration below is a sample chart based on a slight reworking of the spreadsheet created with the INVOICE TaskWizard:

A 3-D Area chart

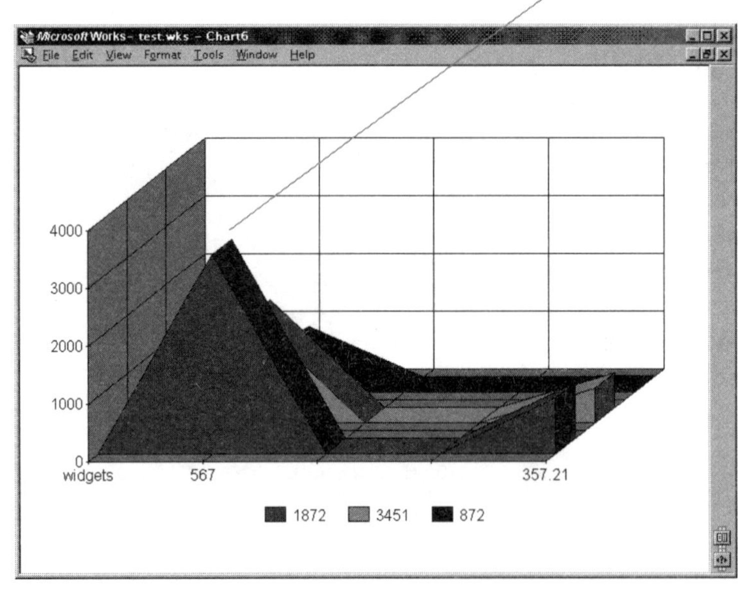

Creating a chart

Select the cells you want to view as a chart. Pull down the Tools menu and click Create New Chart. Carry out steps 1-3 below. Follow steps 4-6 if you need to set advanced chart options. If you didn't follow steps 4-6, carry out step 7.

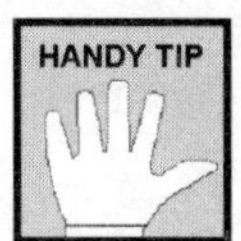

When you select the data cells, include a row or column of text entries if you want these inserted into the chart as descriptive labels.

1 Ensure the Basic Options tab is active

3 Click a chart type

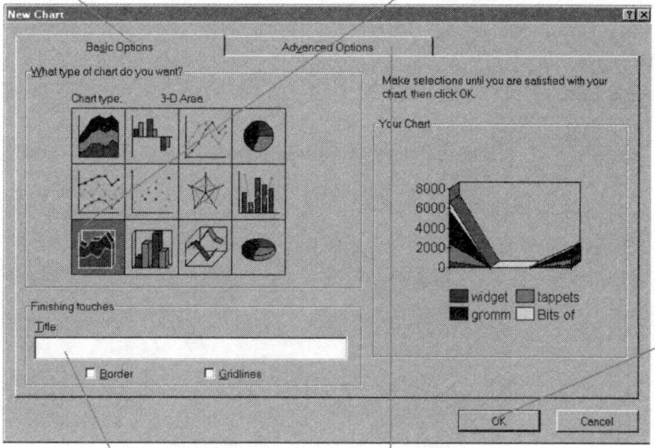

7 Click here

2 Enter a title

4 Click here for Advanced options

5 Click any of these options

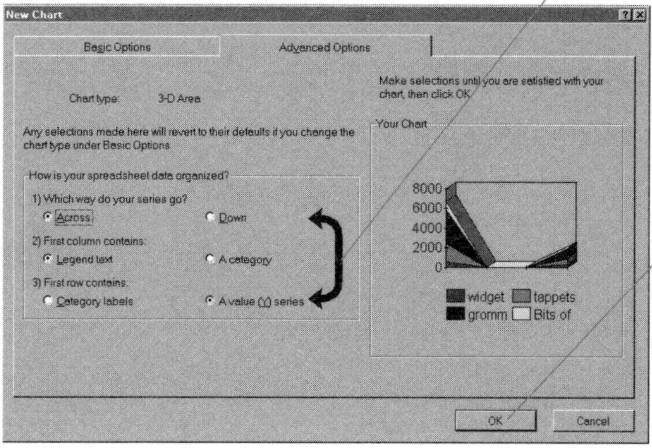

6 Click here

Amending chart formats

Once you've created a chart, you can easily change the underlying chart type. You can also apply a new sub-type.

Each basic chart type has several sub-types (variations) associated with it. These are unavailable when you first create your chart.

Switch to the chart whose format you want to change (if it isn't already open, first follow the procedure in the 'Chart housekeeping' topic to view it). Pull down the Format menu and click Chart Type. Now follow steps 1 and 2. If you want to apply a sub-type, carry out steps 3-5. If you didn't follow steps 3-5, follow step 6.

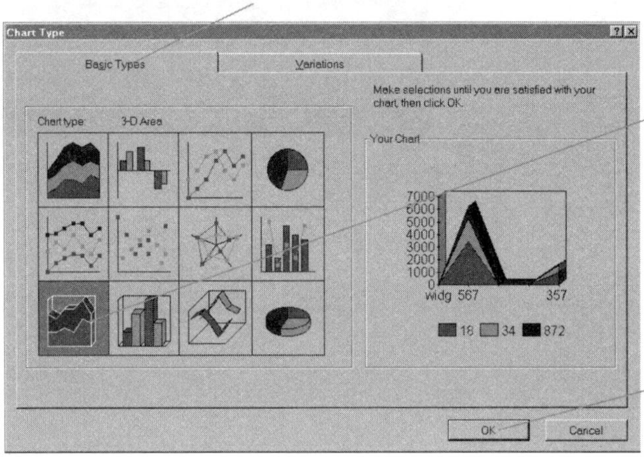

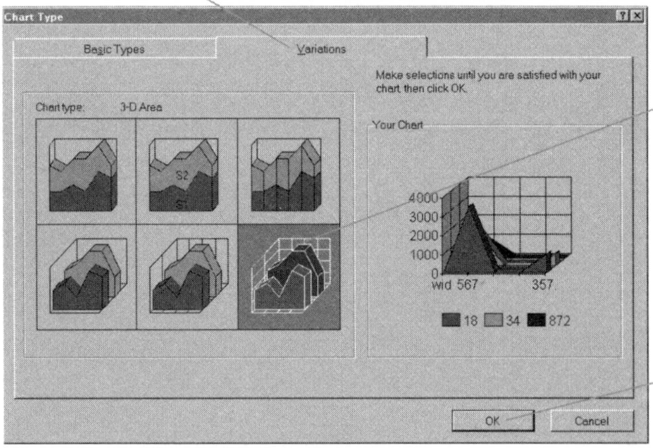

Reformatting charts

You can reformat charts in the following ways. You can:

- apply a new typeface/type size/font style to text

- apply a new colour/shade to graphic components

Reformatting text

Within the open chart, click the text you want to change. Pull down the Format menu and click Font and Style. Carry out any of steps 1-4. Finally, follow step 5.

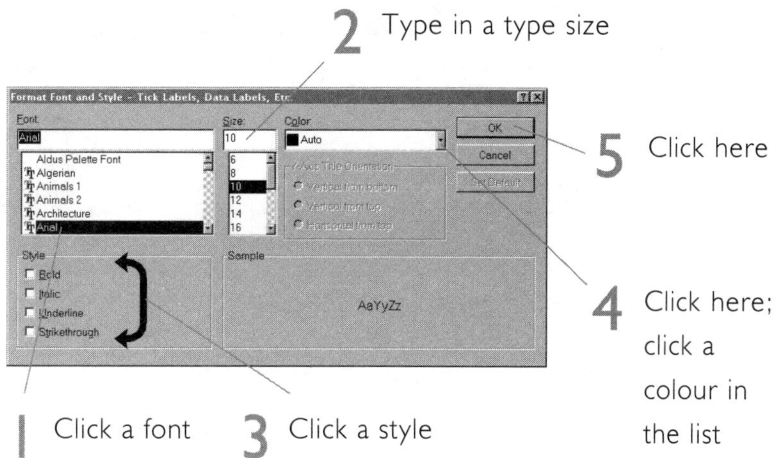

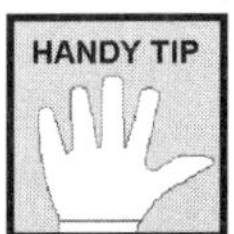

HANDY TIP **The series in a chart are the individual data entries. Below are sample series from a bar chart:**

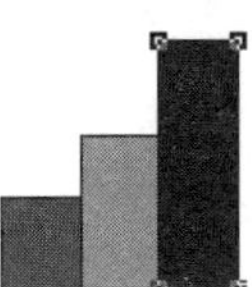

Reformatting graphic objects

Double-click the object (e.g. a series or pie slice) whose colour and/or shading you want to change. Now carry out step 1 or 2 below. Finally, follow step 3.

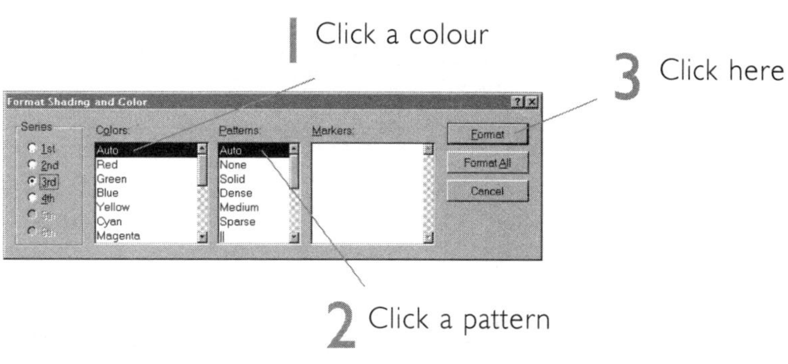

Chart housekeeping

You can't select more than one chart at a time here. To view multiple charts, simply repeat this procedure as often as required.

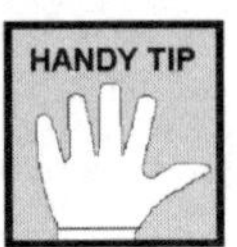

When you've finished working with your chart(s), you can return to the underlying spreadsheet by pulling down the View menu and clicking Spreadsheet.

Viewing charts

A Works spreadsheet can have a maximum of 8 charts associated with it. To view a chart (when the spreadsheet or another chart is on-screen), pull down the View menu and click Chart. Now do the following:

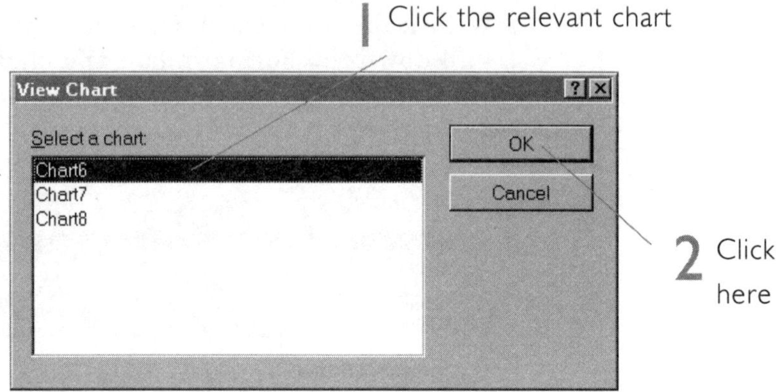

Deleting charts

If you try to create more than 8 charts for a particular spreadsheet, Works will refuse to comply. The answer is to delete one or more earlier charts.

Switch to the chart you want to remove (or follow the procedure above to view it if it isn't already open). Pull down the Tools menu and click Delete Chart. Now do the following:

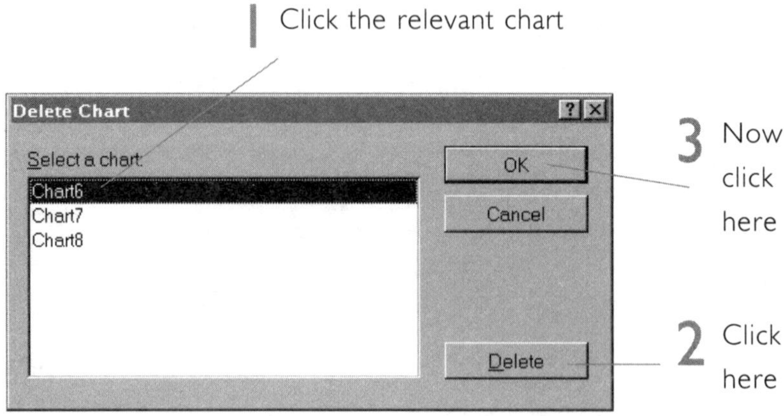

Page setup - an overview

Making sure your spreadsheets print with the correct page setup can be a complex issue, for the simple reason that most become very extensive with the passage of time (so large, in fact, that in the normal course of things they won't fit onto a single page). Luckily, Works makes the entire page setup issue easy.

Page setup features you can customise include:

- the paper size

- the page orientation

- the starting page number

- margins

- whether gridlines are printed

- whether row and column headers are printed

Margin settings you can amend are:

- top

- bottom

- left

- right

Additionally, you can set the distance between the top page edge and the top of the header, and the distance between the bottom page edge and the bottom edge of the footer.

When you save your active spreadsheet, all Page Setup settings are saved with it.

Setting size/orientation options

The Spreadsheet module comes with 11 pre-defined paper types which you can apply to your spreadsheets, in either portrait (top-to-bottom) or landscape (sideways on) orientation.

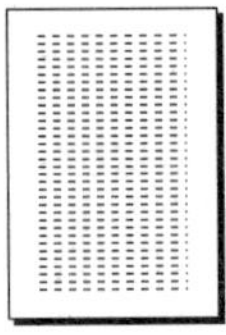

Portrait orientation

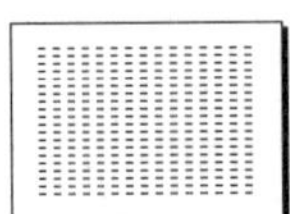

Landscape orientation

If none of the supplied page definitions is suitable, you can create your own.

Applying a new page size/orientation

Pull down the File menu and click Page Setup. Now carry out step 1 below, followed by steps 2-3 as appropriate. Finally, carry out step 4:

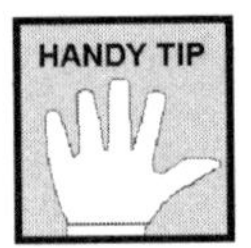

To create your own paper size, click Custom Size in step 3. Then type in the appropriate measurements in the Height & Width fields. Finally, carry out step 4.

Ensure this tab is active

2 Click an orientation

4 Click here

3 Click here; click the page size you need in the drop-down list

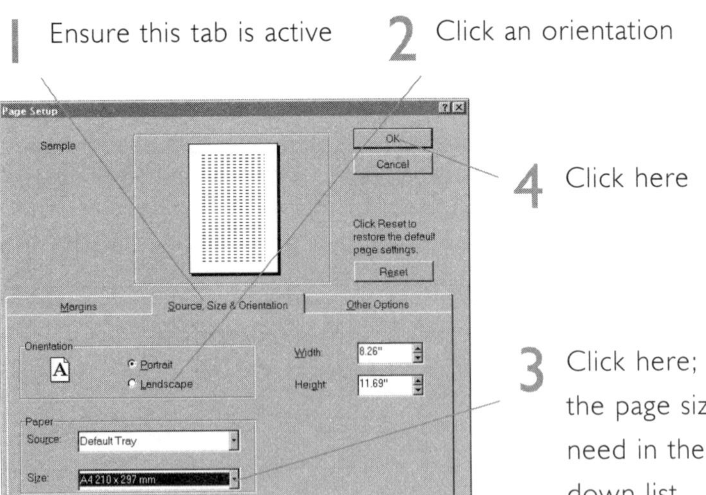

Setting margin options

The Spreadsheet module lets you set a variety of margin settings. The illustration below shows the main ones:

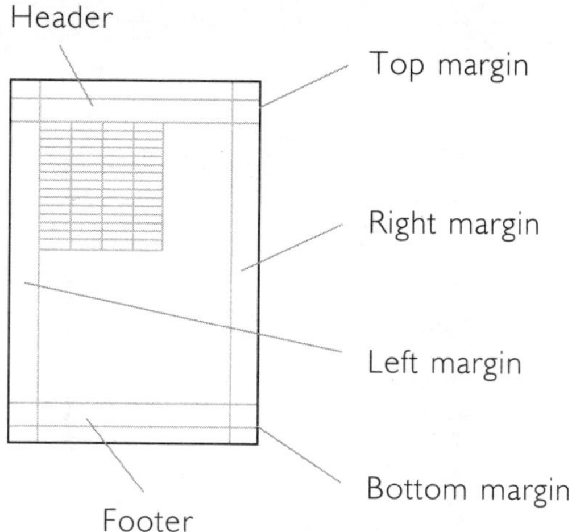

Applying new margins

Pull down the File menu and click Page Setup. Now carry out step 1 below, followed by steps 2-3 as appropriate. Finally, carry out step 4:

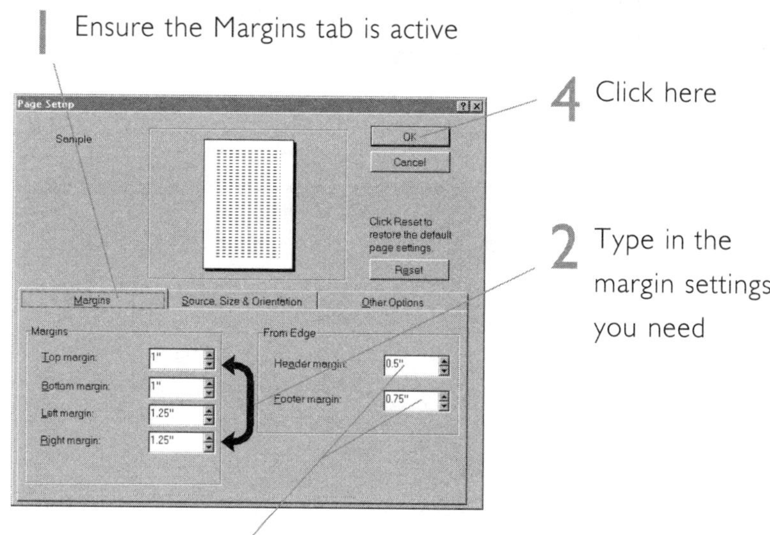

Other page setup options

You can determine whether gridlines and row/column headings print. These are demonstrated below:

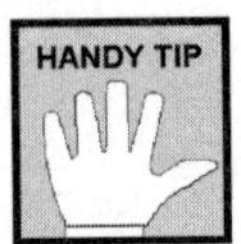

You can also set the page number for the first page in your spreadsheet here (by default, '1') - see below.

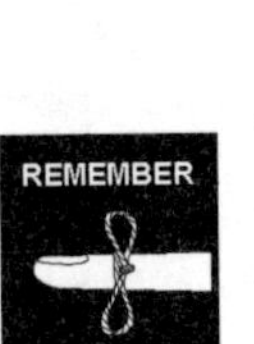

This is an excerpt from the Print Preview screen. For how to use Print Preview in the Spreadsheet, see the 'Using Print Preview' topic later.

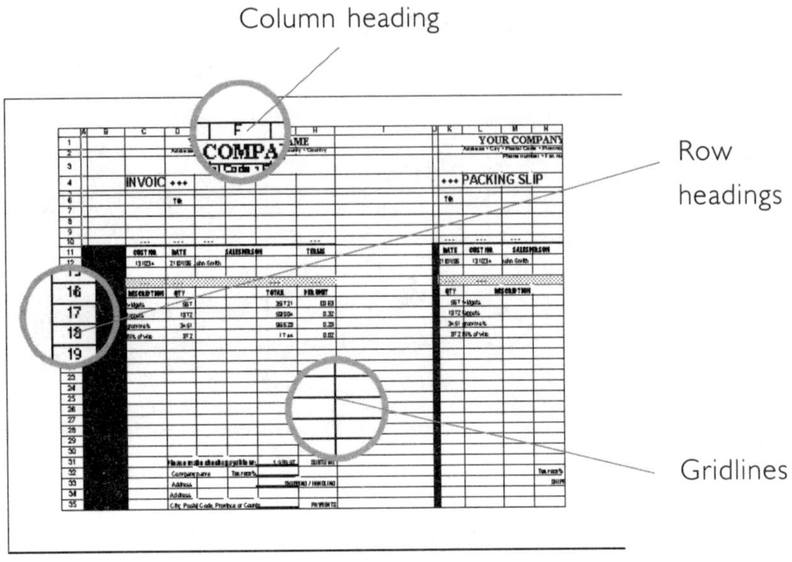

Printing gridlines and row/column headings

Pull down the File menu and click Page Setup. Now carry out step 1 below, followed by steps 2-3 as appropriate. Finally, carry out step 4:

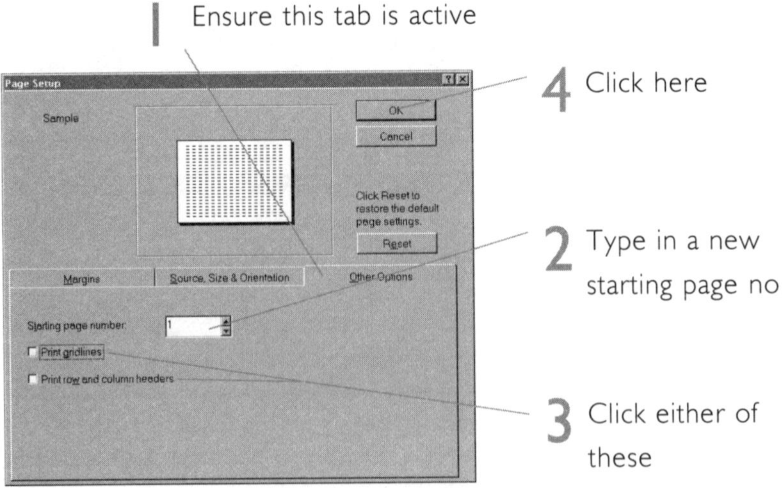

Page setup for charts

Most page setup issues for charts are identical to those for spreadsheet data. However, there are differences. The following additional options are available:

Full page	the chart is expanded to fill the page, with its width/height ratio disrupted, if necessary
Full page, keep proportions	scaled to fit the page, but with its width/height ratio unaltered
Screen size	reduced to the size of your computer screen (so that it occupies roughly 25% of the page)

Customising printed chart sizes

Pull down the File menu and click Page Setup. Now carry out step 1 below, followed by steps 2-3 as appropriate. Finally, carry out step 4:

Ensure this tab is active

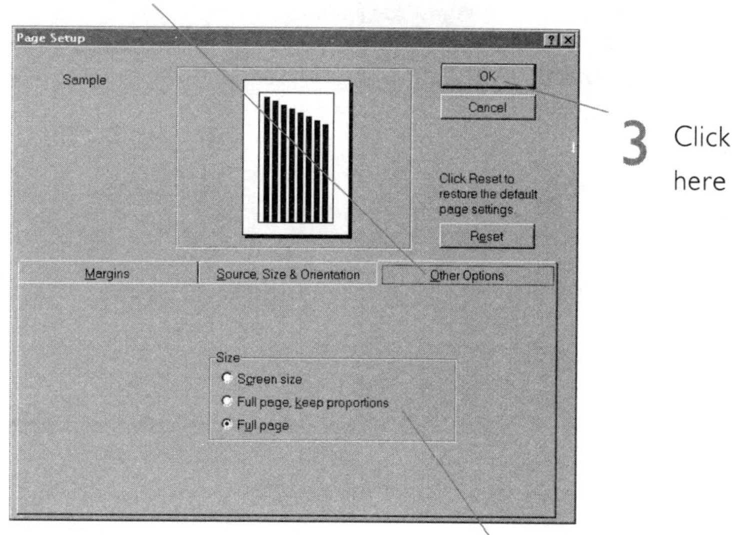

3 Click here

2 Click any scale option

Using Print Preview

The Spreadsheet module provides a special view mode called Print Preview. This displays the active document (one page at a time) exactly as it will look when printed. Use Print Preview as a final check just before you print your document.

When you're using Print Preview, you can zoom in or out on the active page. What you can't do, however, is:

- display more than one page at a time

- edit or revise the active document

Launching Print Preview

Pull down the File menu and click Print Preview. This is the result:

A preview of a chart

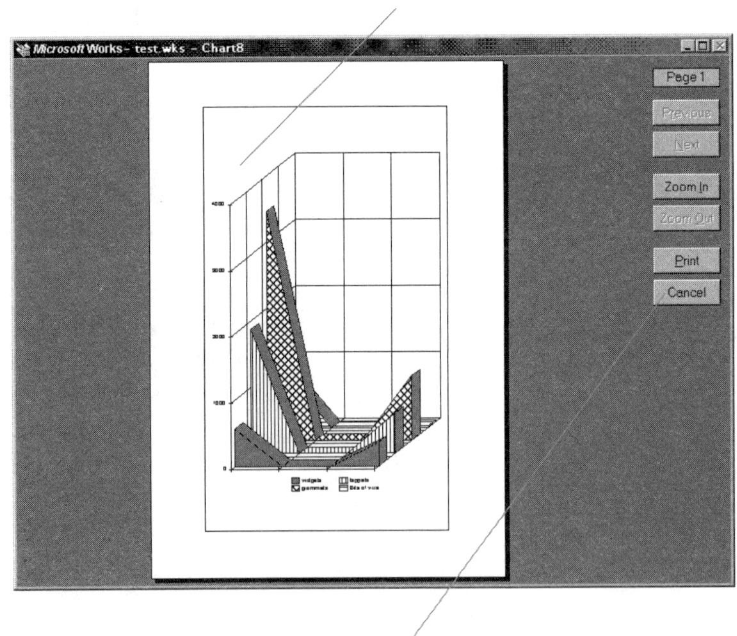

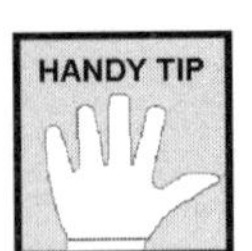

HANDY TIP

You can use a keyboard shortcut to leave Print Preview mode and return to your spreadsheet or chart: simply press Esc.

Click here to leave Print Preview and return to Normal or Page Layout view

Zooming in or out in Print Preview

There are two methods you can use here.

Using the mouse

Move the mouse pointer over the page area; it changes to a magnifying glass. Position this over the portion of the active spreadsheet or chart which you want to expand. Left-click once. Repeat this if necessary.

REMEMBER When you've reached the limit of magnification which Works supports, left-clicking with the mouse *decreases* the magnification.

A magnified view of part of the Print Preview screen

Control Panel

REMEMBER Depending on the current level of magnification, one of the Zoom buttons may be greyed out, and therefore unavailable.

Using the Control Panel

Launch Print Preview. Then carry out the following actions:

Click here to increase the magnification

Click here to decrease the magnification

Changing pages in Print Preview

Although you can only view one page at a time in Print Preview mode, you can step backwards and forwards through the spreadsheet as often as necessary.

There are three methods you can use (in descending order of usefulness).

Using the Control Panel
Carry out the following actions:

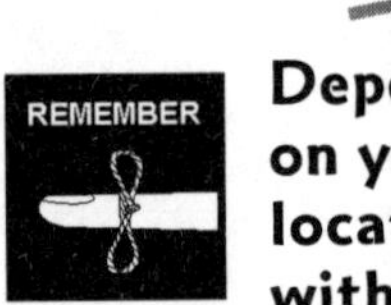

Depending on your location within the document (and the number of pages), one of these buttons may be greyed out, and therefore unavailable.

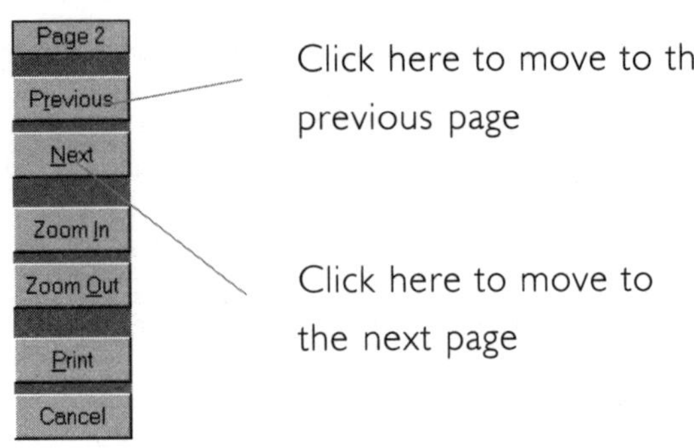

Using the keyboard
You can use the following keyboard shortcuts:

Page Up — Moves to the previous page

Page Down — Moves to the next page

Up cursor — Within a magnified view of a page, moves towards the top of the page

Down cursor — Within a magnified view of a page, moves towards the base of the page

Using the scroll bars
When you're working with a magnified view of a page, use the vertical and/or horizontal scroll bars (using the standard Windows techniques) to move up or down within the page.

Printing spreadsheet data

When you print your data, you can specify:

- the number of copies you want printed

- whether you want the copies 'collated'. This is the process whereby Works prints one full copy at a time. For instance, if you're printing five copies of a 12-page spreadsheet, Works prints pages 1-12 of the first copy, followed by pages 1-12 of the second and pages 1-12 of the third... and so on.

- which pages you want printed

- the printer you want to use (if you have more than one installed on your system)

You can 'mix and match' these, as appropriate.

Starting a print run

Open the spreadsheet which contains the data you want to print. Then pull down the File menu and click Print. Do any of steps 1-4. Then carry out step 5 to begin printing:

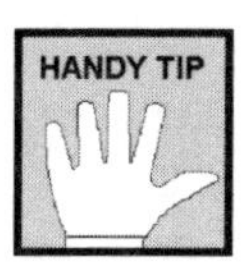

If you need to adjust your printer's internal settings before you initiate printing, click Properties. Then refer to your printer's manual.

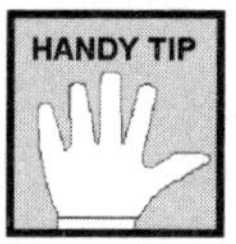

Click Draft quality printing to have your spreadsheet print with minimal formatting.

Click here; select a printer from the list

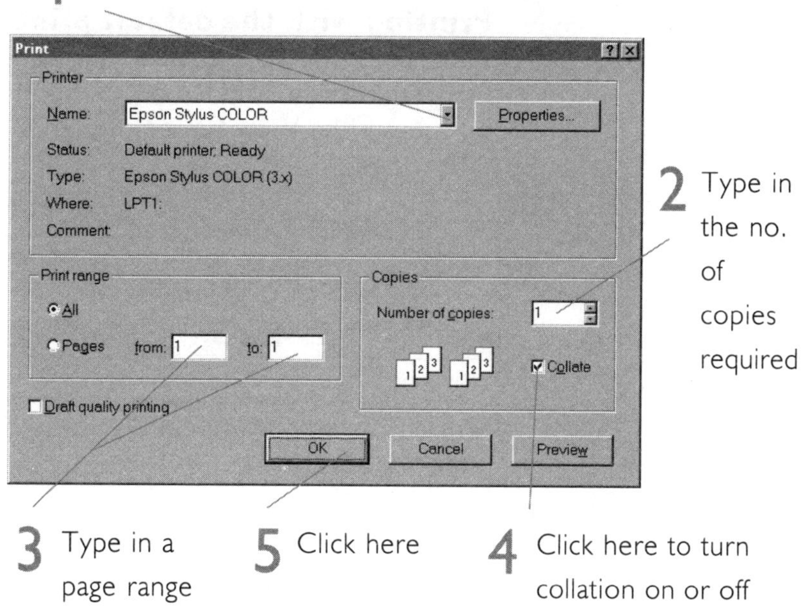

2 Type in the no. of copies required

3 Type in a page range

5 Click here

4 Click here to turn collation on or off

Printing – the fast track approach

In earlier topics, we've looked at how to customise print options to meet varying needs and spreadsheet sizes. However, the Spreadsheet module – like the Word Processor – recognises that there will be times when you won't need this level of complexity. There are occasions when you'll merely want to print out your work – often for proofing purposes – with the standard print defaults applying.

These are:

- Works prints only the active spreadsheet

- Works prints only 1 copy

- Works prints all pages within the active spreadsheet

- collation is turned off

- Works prints with full (not Draft) formatting

For this reason, Works provides a method which bypasses the standard Print dialog, and is therefore much quicker and easier to use.

Printing with the default print options

First, open the spreadsheet you want to print. Ensure your printer is ready. Make sure the toolbar is visible. (If it isn't, pull down the View menu and click Toolbar). Now do the following:

Works starts printing data in the active spreadsheet immediately.

The Database

This chapter gives you the fundamentals of using the Database module. You'll learn how to work with data and formulas, and how to move around through databases. You'll also learn how to locate data, and apply formatting to make it more visually effective. Finally, you'll customise page layout/printing.

Covers

The Database screen

Below is a detailed illustration of a typical Database screen.

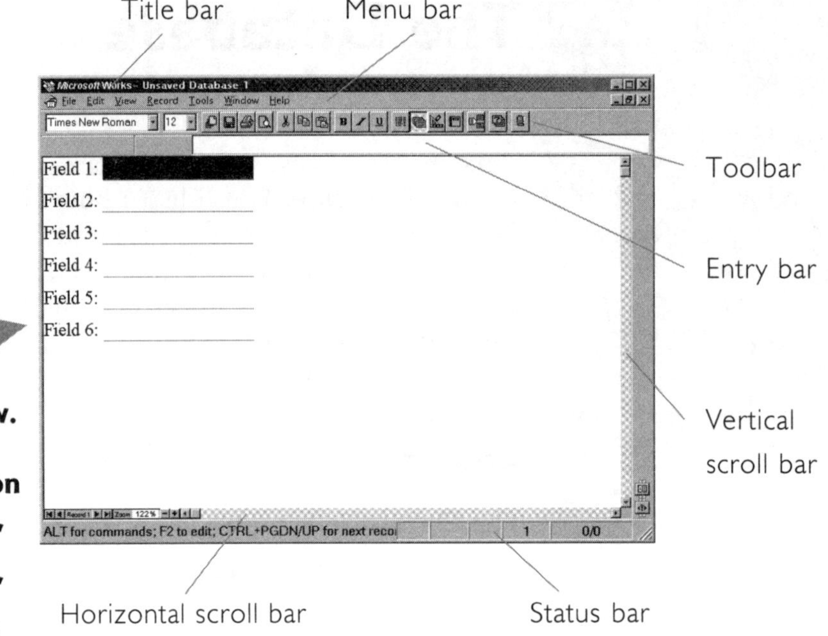

This is Form view. For more information on Database views, see the 'Using Database views (1)' & 'Using Database views (2)' topics later.

Some of these – e.g. the rulers and scroll bars – are standard to just about all programs which run under Windows. One – the toolbar – can be hidden, if required.

Specifying whether the toolbar displays

Pull down the View menu. Then do the following:

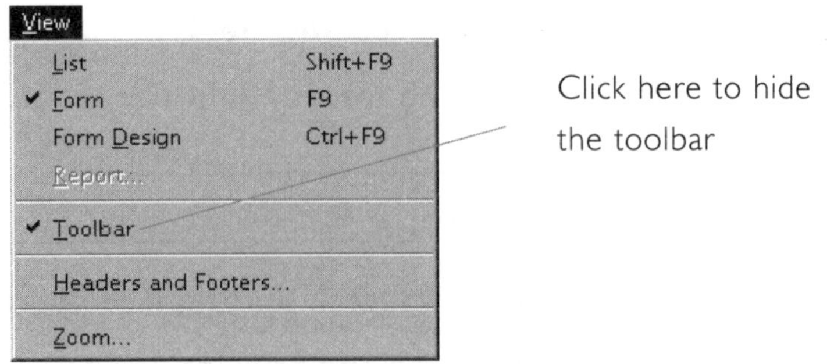

Click here to hide the toolbar

Creating your first database

See the 'Creating blank documents' topic in Section 1 for how to use the Task Launcher to create a new Database document.

Unlike the Word Processor and Spreadsheet modules, the Database *doesn't* create a new blank document immediately after you've launched it from within the Task Launcher. Instead, you have to complete several dialogs first. Do the following:

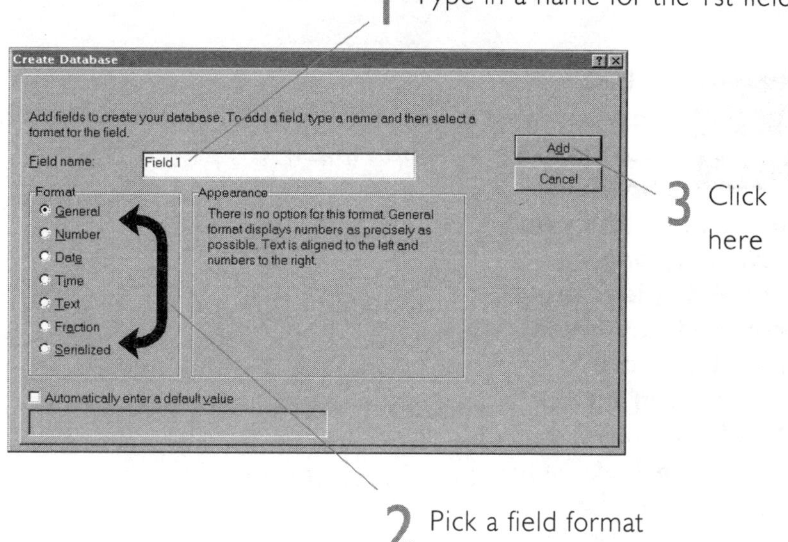

Database fields are single columns of information (in List view) or spaces for the insertion of information (in Form view).

After you've followed step 3, Works produces the same dialog so that you can create the second field. Repeat the above procedures as often as necessary. When you've defined your final field, do the following:

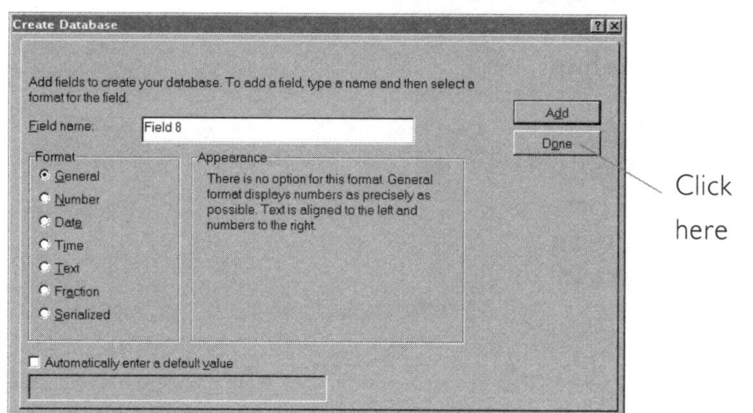

Entering data (1)

When you've created a database, you can begin entering data immediately. You can enter the following basic data types:

- numbers

- text

- functions

- formulas (combinations of numbers, text and functions)

You enter data into 'fields'. Fields are organised into 'records'. Records are whole units of related information.

To understand this, we'll take a specific example. In an address book, the categories under which information is entered (e.g. 'Surname', 'Address', 'Phone No.') are fields, while each person whose details are entered into the database constitutes one record. This is shown in the next illustration:

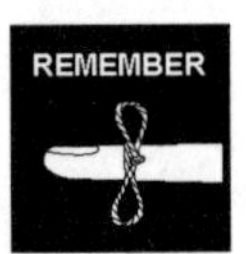

In List view, records are shown as single rows. In Form view, only one record displays on-screen at any given time. For more information on Database views, see the 'Using Database views (1)' & 'Using Database views (2)' topics later.

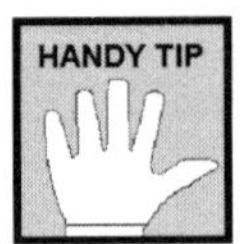

This is List view. List view is suitable for the mass insertion of data (more than 1 record is visible at a time). However, you can also enter data in Form view.

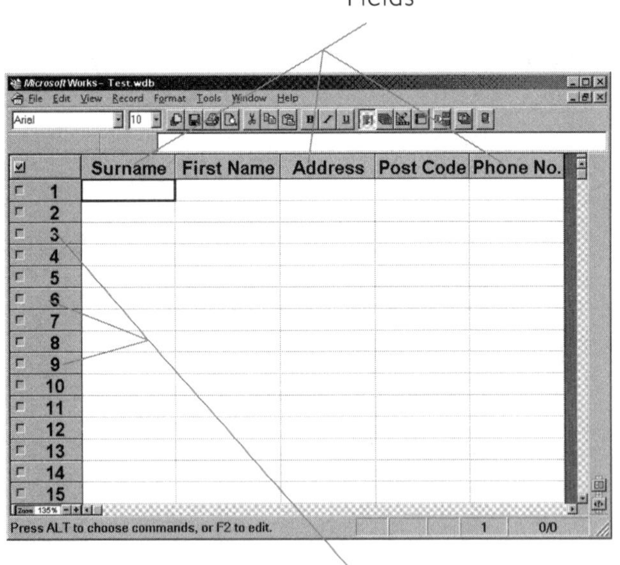

Entering data (2)

Although you can enter data *directly* into a database field (by simply clicking in it and typing it in), there's another method you can use which is often easier. Like the Spreadsheet module, the Database provides a special screen component known as the Entry bar.

In the illustration below, two fields in the first record have been completed.

Entry bar

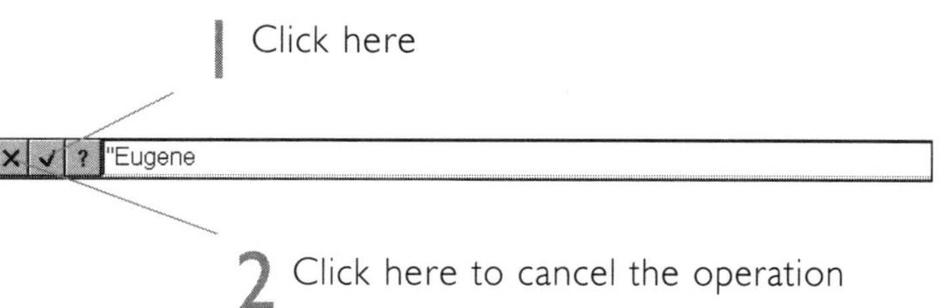

Entering data via the Entry bar

Click the field you want to insert data into. Then click the Entry bar. Type in the data. Then follow step 1 below. If you decide not to proceed with the operation, follow step 2 instead:

> **HANDY TIP**
>
> **You can use a keyboard route to confirm operations in the Entry bar: simply press Return.**

Modifying existing data

You can amend the contents of a field in two ways:

- via the Entry bar

- from within the field

When you use either of these methods, the Database enters a special state known as Edit Mode.

Amending existing data using the Entry bar

Click the field whose contents you want to change. Then click in the Entry bar. Make the appropriate revisions and/ or additions. Then press Return. The relevant field is updated.

Amending existing data internally

Click the field whose contents you want to change. Press F2. Make the appropriate revisions and/or additions *within the field*. Then press Return.

The illustration below shows our new database, in Form view.

A magnified view of the Address field in the

first record of our database, in Edit Mode

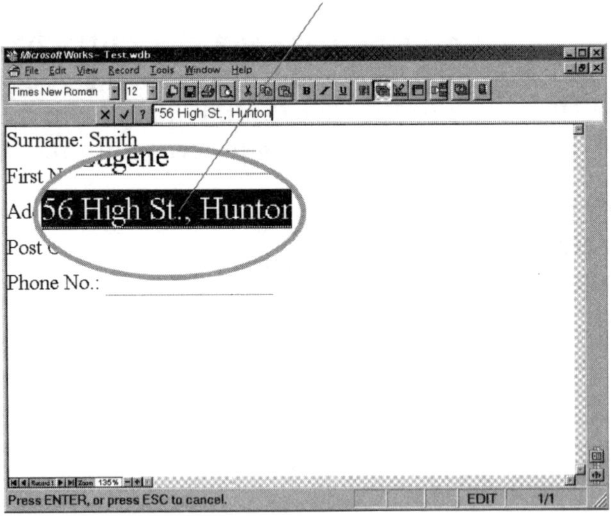

Using Database views (1)

The Database module provides two principal views:

List

List view presents your data in a grid structure reminiscent of the Spreadsheet module, with the columns denoting fields and the rows individual records. Pictures and most formatting components do not display.

Use List view for bulk data entry or comparison.

Form

Form view limits the display to one record at a time, while presenting it in a way which is more visual and therefore easier on the eye. The basis of this view is the 'form', the underlying database layout which you can customise in Form Design view. Pictures and formatting display in Form view (although you can only initiate them in Form Design view).

In many circumstances, Form view provides the best way to interact with your database.

A third view - Form Design view - is a subset of Form view.

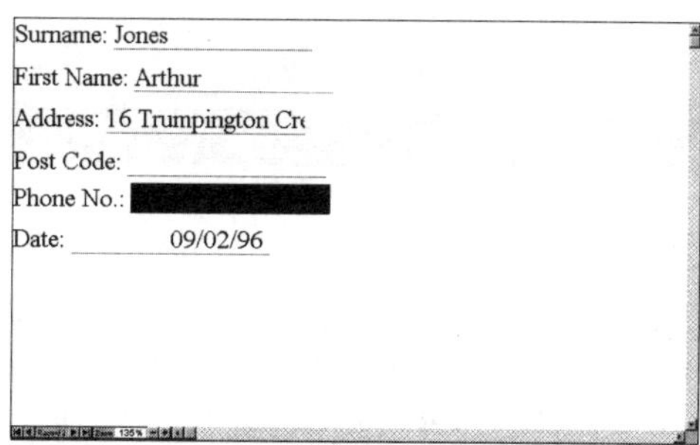

A database in Form view...

	Surname	First Name	Address	Post
1	Smith	Eugene	56 High St., Hunton	
2	Jones	Arthur	16 Trumpington Cres., Camford	
3	Brown	Inigo	12 Codwalleder Ave. Slipforth	
4				
5				
6				
7				
8				
9				
10				
11				
12				
13				
14				
15				

And in List view

Using Database views (2)

You can use three methods to switch to another view.

The menu approach...

Pull down the View menu and do the following:

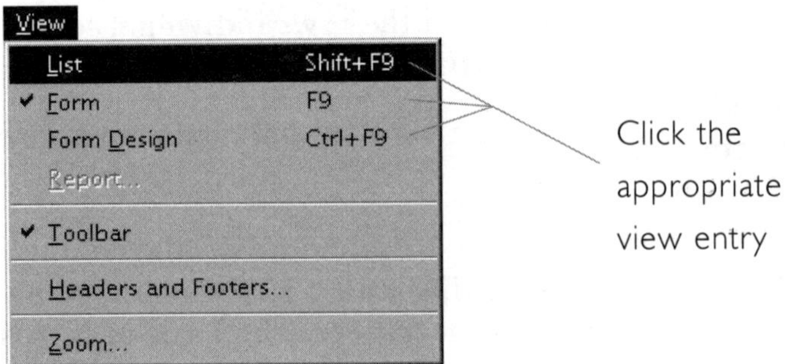

Click the appropriate view entry

The toolbar approach...

Make sure the toolbar is visible. (If it isn't, pull down the View menu and click Toolbar). Now click one of the following:

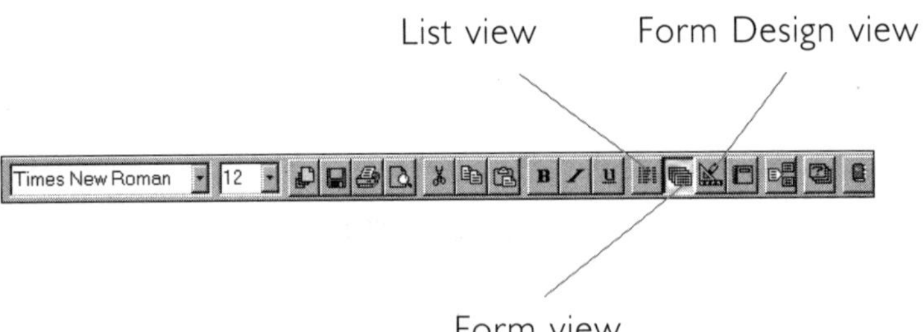

The keyboard approach...

Use any of the following combinations:

F9	Form view
Shift+F9	List view
Ctrl+F9	Form Design view

Moving around in databases (1)

Databases can quickly become very large. The Database module provides several techniques you can use to find your way round.

Using the scroll bars

Use any of the following methods:

1. To scroll quickly to another record (in List view) or to another field (in Form view), drag the scroll box along the scroll bar until you reach it.

2. To move one window to the right or left, click to the left or right of the scroll box in the horizontal scroll bar.

3. To move one window up or down, click above or below the scroll box in the vertical scroll bar.

4. To move up or down by one record (in List view) or one field (in Form view), click the arrows in the vertical scroll bar.

5. To move left or right by one field, click the arrows in the horizontal scroll bar.

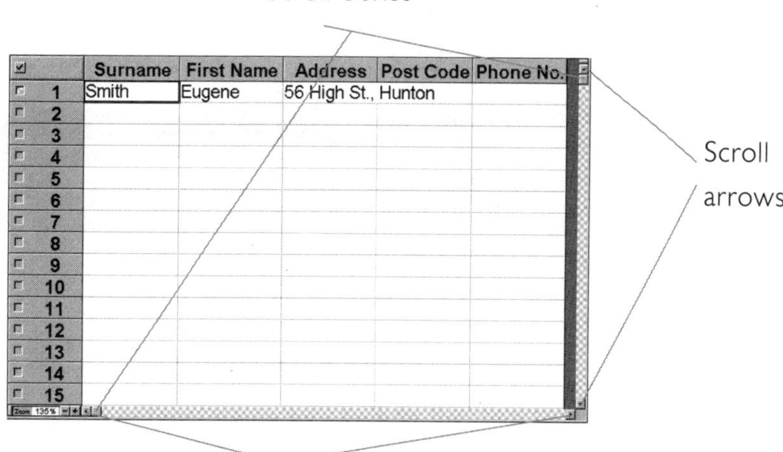

Moving around in databases (2)

Using the keyboard

You can use the following techniques:

1. In List view, use the cursor keys to move one field left, right, up or down. In Form view, use the up and left cursor keys to move one field up, or the down and right keys to move one field down.

2. Press Home to jump to the first field in the active record, or End to move to the last.

3. Press Ctrl+Home to move to the first record in the open database, or Ctrl+End to move to the last.

4. Press Page Up or Page Down to move up or down by one screen.

5. In Form view, press Ctrl+Page Down to move to the next record, or Ctrl+Page Up to move to the previous one.

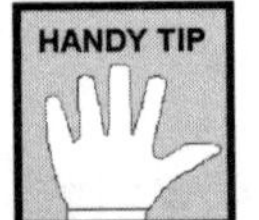

You can use a keyboard shortcut to launch the Go To dialog: simply press F5, or Ctrl+G.

Using the Go To dialog

The Database provides a special dialog which you can use to specify precise field or record destinations.

Pull down the Edit menu and click Go To. Now carry out step 1 or 2 below. Finally, follow step 3.

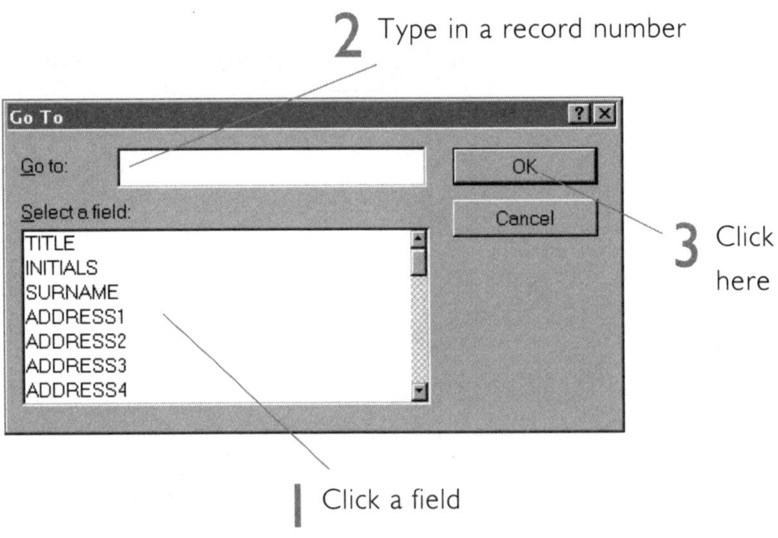

Using Zoom (1)

The ability to vary the level of magnification in the Database module is very useful. Sometimes, it's helpful to 'zoom out' (i.e. decrease the magnification) so that you can take an overview; at other times, you'll need to 'zoom in' (increase the magnification) to work in greater detail. Works makes this process easy and convenient.

You can change magnification levels in the Database module:

- with the use of the Zoom area

- with the Zoom dialog

Using the Zoom area

You can use the Zoom area (at the base of the screen) to alter zoom levels with the minimum of effort. Carry out step 1 or 2, or steps 3&4, as appropriate:

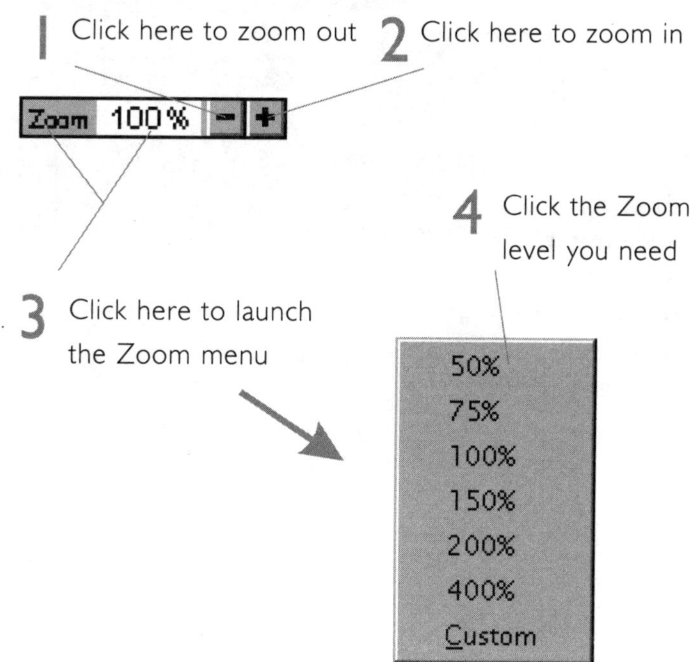

HANDY TIP

Re step 4 - clicking Custom produces the Zoom dialog. See the 'Using Zoom (2)' topic for how to use this.

Using Zoom (2)

Using the Zoom dialog

Using the Zoom dialog, you can perform either of the following:

- choose from preset zoom levels (e.g. 400%, 200%, 50%)

- specify your own zoom percentage

If you want to impose your own, custom zoom level, it's probably easier, quicker and more convenient to use the Zoom dialog.

Pull down the View menu and click Zoom. Now carry out step 1 or 2 below. Finally, follow step 3.

Entries here must lie in the range 33%-1000%.

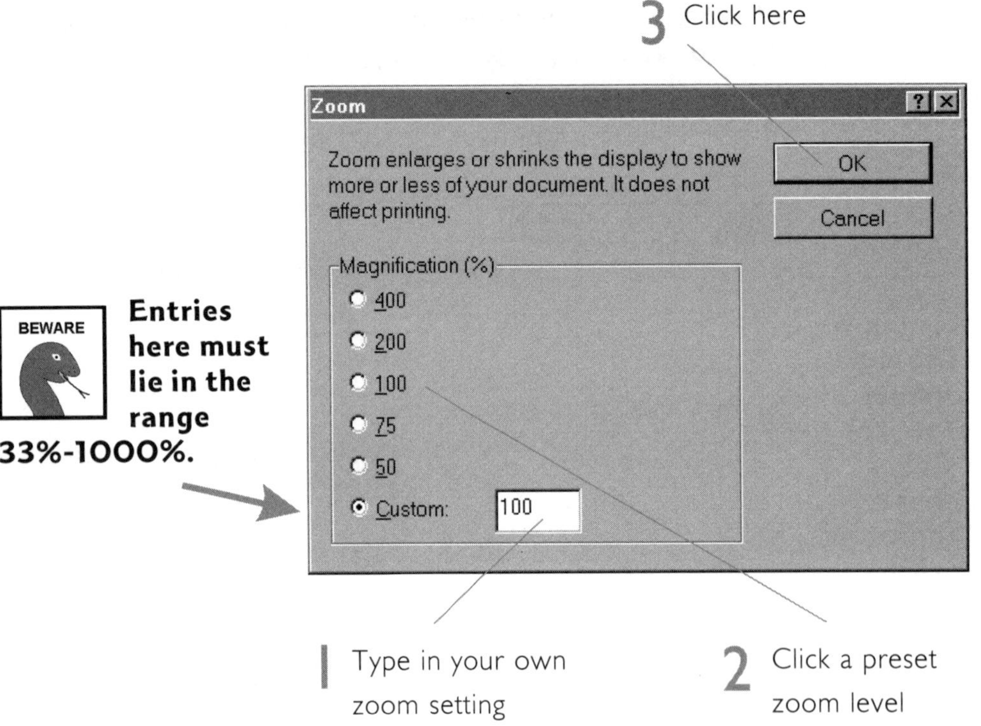

Selection techniques in List view

Before you can carry out any editing operations on fields or records in the Database module, you have to select them first. The available selection techniques vary according to whether you're currently using List or Form view.

Follow any of the techniques below:

Using the mouse

To select a single field	Simply click in it.
To select multiple fields	Click the field in the top left-hand corner; hold down the mouse button and drag over the fields you want to highlight. Release the mouse button.
To select one record	Click the record number.
To select multiple records	Hold down Shift as you click the record numbers.

REMEMBER **With the exception of the first, selected fields are filled with black.**

☑		Surname	First Name	Address	Post Code	Phone No.
☐	1	Smith	Eugene	56 High St., Hunton		
☐	2	Jones	Arthur	16 Trumping	Camford	
☐	3	Brown	Inigo	12 Codwalleder Ave.	Slipforth	

Record numbers

Using the keyboard

To select multiple fields	Position the insertion point in the first field. Press F8. Use the cursor keys to extend the selection area. Press F8 when you've finished.
To select a whole record	Position the insertion point in the record. Press Ctrl+F8.
To select a whole field	Position the insertion point in the field. Press Shift+F8.

HANDY TIP **To select the whole of the active database in List view, press Ctrl+Shift+F8.**

Selection techniques in forms

Note that some of the techniques discussed here **(they're clearly marked) will only work in Form Design view.**

These arrow buttons can be found in the bottom left-hand corner of the Form view screen.

Using the mouse

To select a single field	Simply click in it.
To select multiple fields	Hold down Ctrl as you click in successive fields (you must be in Form Design view to do this).
To select one record	Do any of the following:

Move to previous record   Jump to final record

Jump to first record   Move to next record

To select multiple field names or inserted pictures	In Form Design view, hold down Ctrl as you click on successive objects.

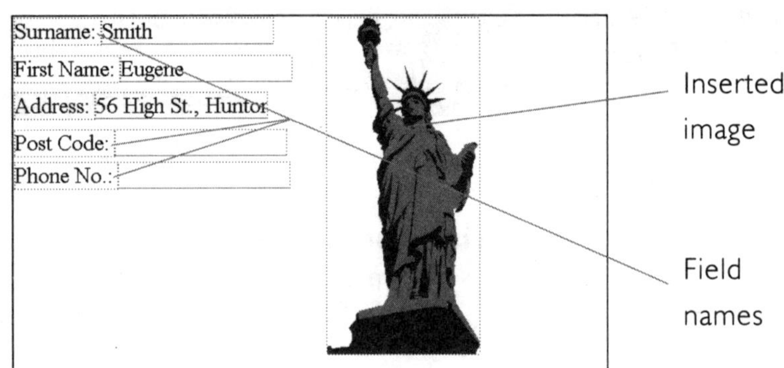

Using the keyboard

To select a field	Use the cursor keys to position the insertion point in the relevant field.
To select a record	Press Ctrl+Page Up or Ctrl+Page Down until the record you want is displayed.

Formulas - an overview

You can insert formulas into Database fields. Formulas in the Database module work in much the same way as in the Spreadsheet. However, there are fewer applications for them.

Database formulas serve two principal functions:

- to ensure that the same entry appears in a given field throughout every record in a database

- to return a value based on the contents of multiple additional fields

Look at the next illustration:

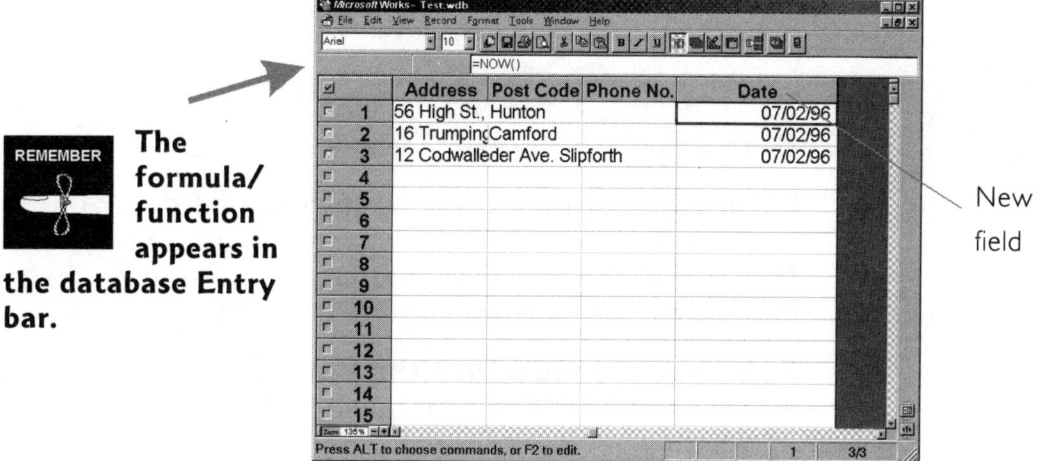

The formula/ function appears in the database Entry bar.

New field

Here, an extra field has been added (see later for how to do this) and a formula (in this case, consisting entirely of a function) inserted. The function

=NOW()

inserts the current system date in the Date field within every record.

Inserting a formula

Arguments (e.g. field references) relating to functions are always contained in brackets.

As in the Spreadsheet module, all Database formulas must begin with an equals sign. This is usually followed by a permutation of the following:

- one or more operands (in the case of the Database module, field names)

- a function (e.g. AVG – returns the Average)

- an arithmetical operator (+, –, /, * and ^)

The Database supports a very wide assortment of functions. For more information on how to insert functions, refer to the 'Inserting a function' topic.

The arithmetical operators are (in the order in which they appear in the bulleted list above):

plus, minus, divide, multiply and *exponential.*

There are two ways to enter formulas:

Entering a formula directly into the field

Click the field into which you want to insert a formula. Then type =, followed by your formula. When you've finished defining the formula, press Return.

Entering a formula into the Entry bar

This is usually the most convenient method.

Click the field in which you want to insert a formula. Then click in the Entry bar. Type =, followed by your formula. When you've finished defining the formula, press Return or do the following:

Click here

| X | ✓ | ? | =NOW() |

Database functions

In many ways, the Database module's implementation of functions parallels that of the Spreadsheet module. However, there is one important difference: you can't use Easy Calc to insert them. Instead, you have to do so manually. Luckily, though, the inbuilt HELP system provides assistance.

Using HELP before you insert a function

Pull down the Help menu and click Contents. Now do the following:

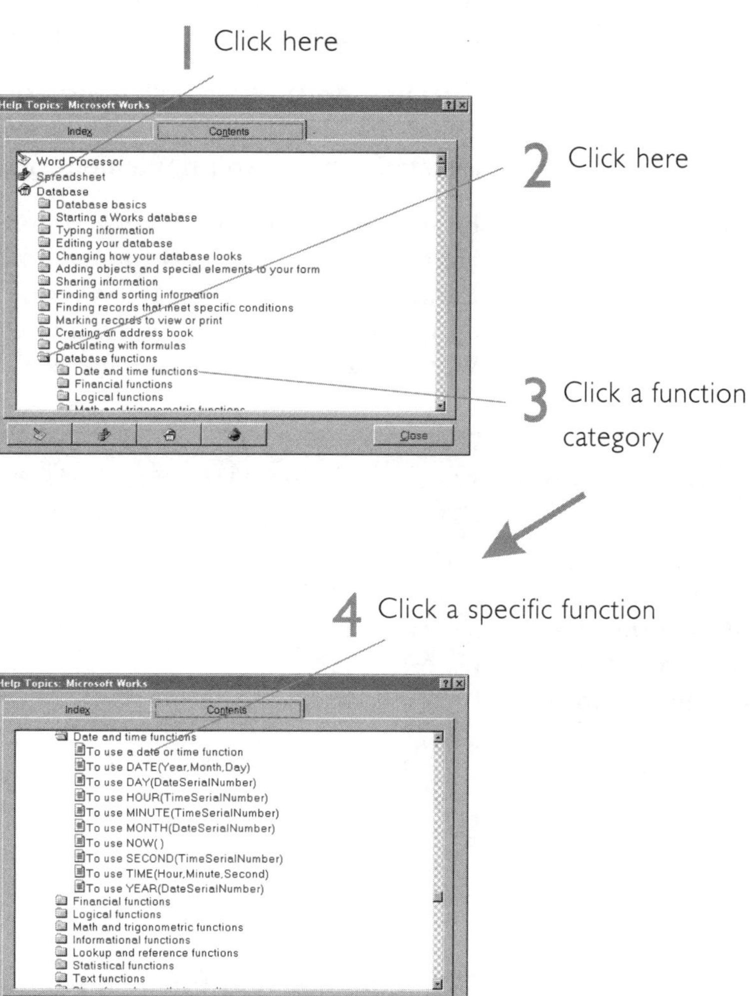

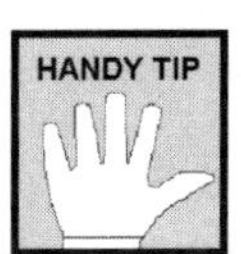

After you've followed step 4, Works launches a HELP window with function-specific assistance.

Inserting a function

There are two ways to insert functions:

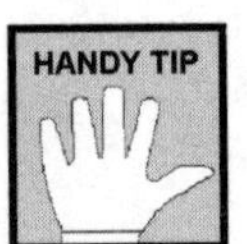

See 'Further help with inserting functions' below for how to complete function arguments.

Entering a function directly into the field

Click the field into which you want to insert the function. Type = followed by the function itself. Finally, press Return to confirm the operation.

Entering a function into the Entry bar

Click the field in which you want to insert the function. Then click in the Entry bar. Type = followed by your function. When you've finished defining the function, press Return or click ✔ in the Entry bar.

Further help with inserting functions

The Works on-line HELP system provides additional assistance when you implement functions.

First, ensure the HELP window is currently displayed. (If it isn't, click ⟨⟩ in the bottom right-hand corner of the Database screen). Then follow either of the procedures outlined above. When you type in the function name, Works launches a special function window:

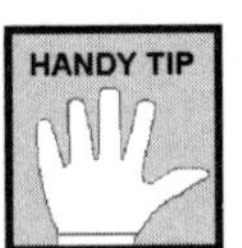

The HELP window provides syntax guidance for the specific function you want to enter.

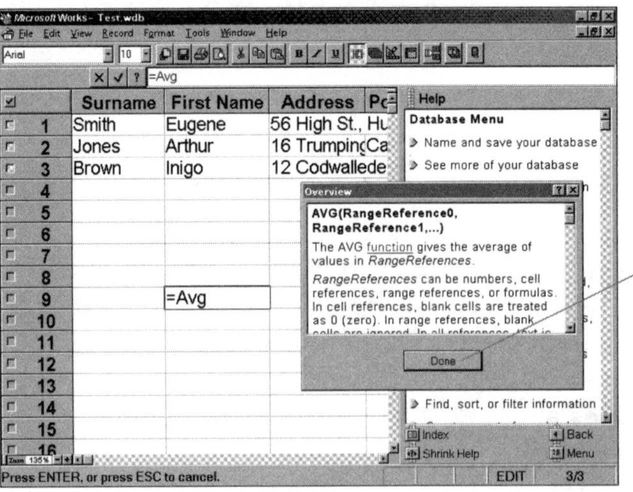

Click here when you've finished using HELP

Now complete your function's arguments in the normal way.

Inserting fields

You can add one or more blank fields to the active database, from within either List or Form Design (but not Form) view.

Adding a field in Form Design view

If you're not already in Form Design view, pull down the View menu and click Form Design. Click where you want the new field inserted. Pull down the Insert menu and click Field.

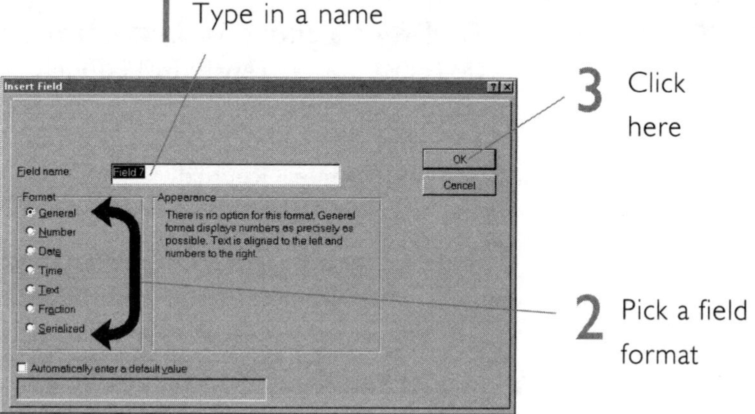

Adding one or more fields in List view

If you're not currently in List view, pull down the View menu and click List. Click in the field next to which you want the new field(s) added. Pull down the Record menu and click Insert Field. In the sub-menu, click Before or After, as appropriate.

Repeat this procedure to add as many additional fields as necessary.

The Insert Field dialog launches. Follow steps 1-3 above. The dialog now changes. Do *either* of the following:

1.   Click Done to add the single field and close the dialog.

2.   Carry out steps 1-3 again to add a further field.

If you carried out 2, click Done when you've added the correct number of new fields.

Inserting records

You can add one or more blank records to the active database, from within either List or Form (but not Form Design) view.

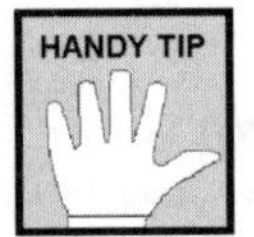

See the 'Moving around in databases (2)' topic earlier for how to jump to the relevant record.

Adding a record in Form view

If you're not already in Form view, pull down the View menu and click Form. Go to the record before which you want the new record to appear. Pull down the Record menu and click Insert Record.

Adding a record in List view

If you're not currently in List view, pull down the View menu and click List. Click in the record above which you want the new record added. Pull down the Record menu and click Insert Record.

If you select more than one existing record, Works inserts the equivalent number of new records.

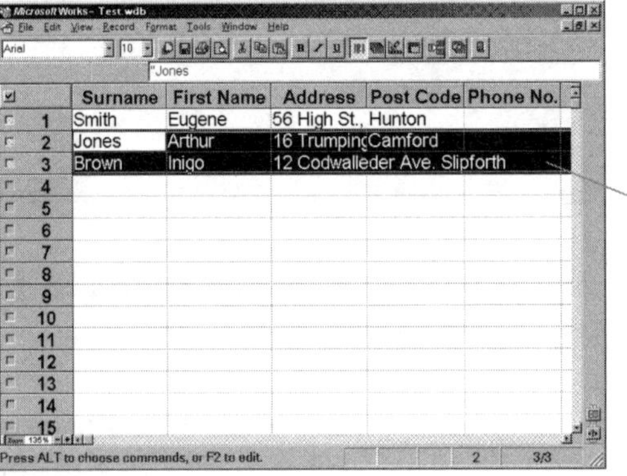

Preparing to add two new records in List view...

The records have been added

Amending record/field sizes

Sooner or later, you'll find it necessary to change the dimensions of fields or records within List view. This necessity arises when there is too much data to display adequately. You can enlarge or shrink single or multiple fields/records.

Changing record height

To change one record's height, click the record number. If you want to change multiple records, hold down Shift and click the appropriate extra numbers. Then pull down the Format menu and click Record Height. Carry out the following steps:

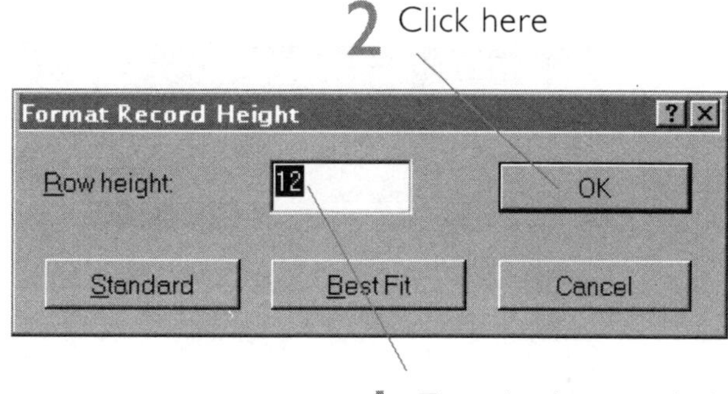

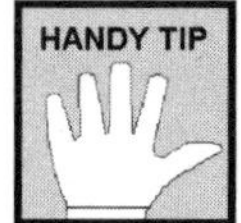

Works has a useful 'best fit' feature. Simply click Best Fit in either dialog to have the record(s) or field(s) adjust themselves automatically to their contents.

Changing field widths

To change one field's width, click the field heading. If you want to change multiple fields, hold down Shift and click the appropriate extra headings. Then pull down the Format menu and click Field Width. Now do the following:

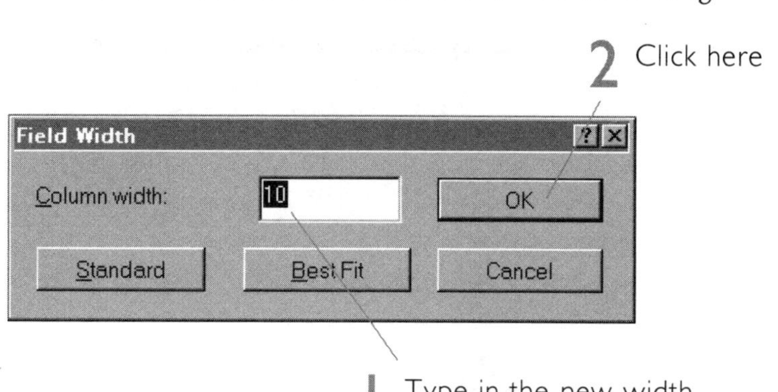

Working with fills

In List view, you can have the contents of a selected field entry automatically copied into other field entries or records.

Use this technique to save time and effort.

Duplicating a field entry

Click the field entry whose contents you want to duplicate. Then move the mouse pointer over the appropriate border. Click and hold down the button; drag the border over the field entries or records into which you want the contents inserted. Release the button.

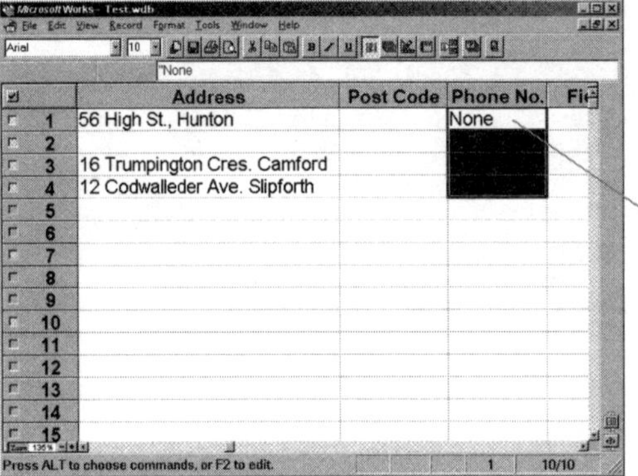

In this illustration, the contents of the Phone No. field in record 1 are to be copied into the same field entries in records 2-4

Now pull down the Edit menu and click Fill Right or Fill Down, as appropriate.

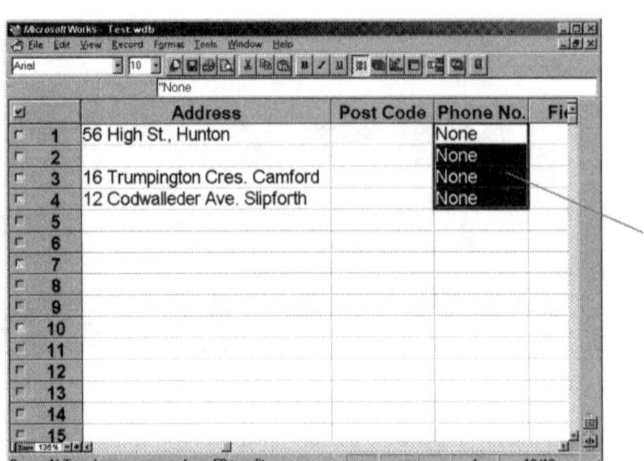

The fill operation has been completed

Working with fill series

You can also carry out fills which *extrapolate* field entry contents over the specified entries. Look at the next illustration:

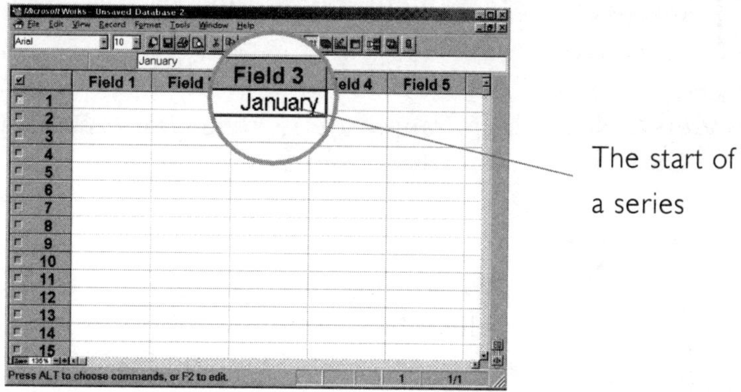

The start of a series

If (as here) you wanted to insert month names in successive field entries, you could do so manually. But there's a much easier way. You can have Works do it for you.

Creating a series

REMEMBER

Re step 2 - the step value sets the rate by which the series increments (plus numbers) or decrements (minus numbers). For example, setting -2 in this instance would produce the following series: 'November, September, July, May...'.

Type in the first element(s) of the series in consecutive field entries. Select the entries. Then pull down the Edit menu and click Fill Series. Now do the following:

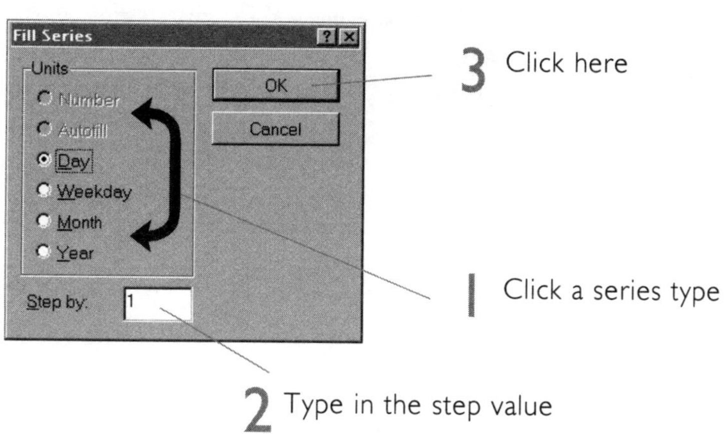

3 Click here

1 Click a series type

2 Type in the step value

Changing fonts and styles

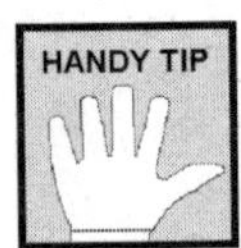

You can carry out any of these from within List or Form Design views. Note, however, that the results are independent - e.g. you can colour the same field red in Form Design view and blue in List view.

The Database module lets you carry out the following actions on field contents (numbers, text or combinations of both):

- apply a new font

- apply a new type size

- apply a font style (*Italic*, **Bold**, <u>Underlining</u> or ~~Strikethrough~~)

- apply a colour

Amending the appearance of field contents

Select the data you want to reformat. Pull down the Format menu and click Font and Style. Carry out step 1 below. Now follow any of steps 2-5, as appropriate. Finally, carry out step 6.

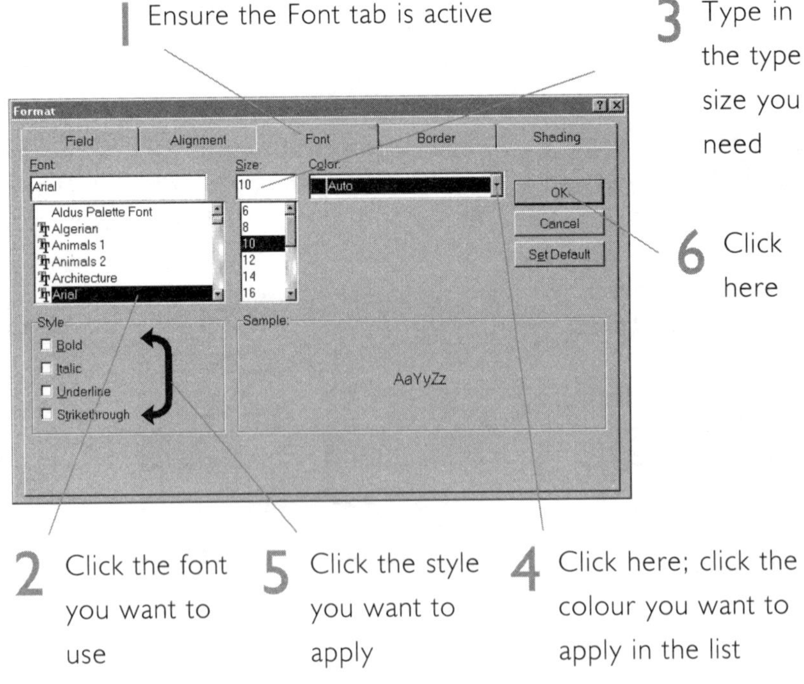

Aligning field contents

You can apply the following alignments to field entries:

The full alignment options are only available within List view.

Horizontal alignment

General	the default (text to the left, numbers to the right)
Left	contents are aligned from the left
Right	contents are aligned from the right
Center	contents are centred

Vertical alignment

Top	contents align with the top of the field(s)
Center	contents are centred
Bottom	contents align with the field bottom

Customising alignment & applying text wrap

Select the relevant field(s). Pull down the Format menu and click Alignment. Carry out step 1. Now follow any or all of steps 2-4, as appropriate. Finally, carry out step 5.

When text wrap is selected, any surplus text within a field is forced onto separate lines. Note that text wrap is only available within List view.

Ensure the Alignment tab is active

5 Click here

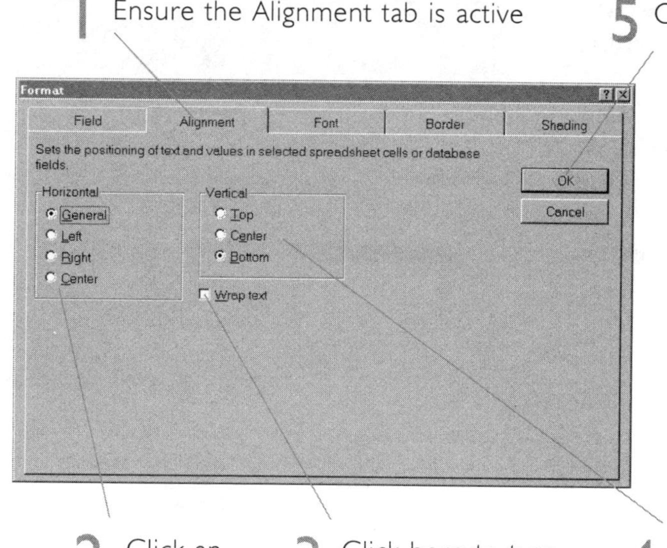

2 Click an alignment

3 Click here to turn on text wrap

4 Click an alignment

Bordering fields

In List view, you can define a border around:

You can border fields in Form Design view, too. However, you can only create perimeter borders.

- the perimeter of selected field(s)

- the individual fields *within* a group of selected fields

- specific field sides

You can customise the border by choosing from a selection of pre-defined border styles. You can also colour it, if required.

Applying a field border

First, click the heading(s) of the field(s) you want to border. Pull down the Format menu and click Border. Now carry out steps 1 and 2 below. Step 3 is optional. Finally, follow steps 4 and 5. If you're setting multiple border options, repeat steps 2-4 as required.

Re step 4 – Outline borders the perimeter of the selected field(s). The other options (you can click more than 1) affect *individual* sides.

1 Ensure the Border tab is active

2 Click the relevant line style option

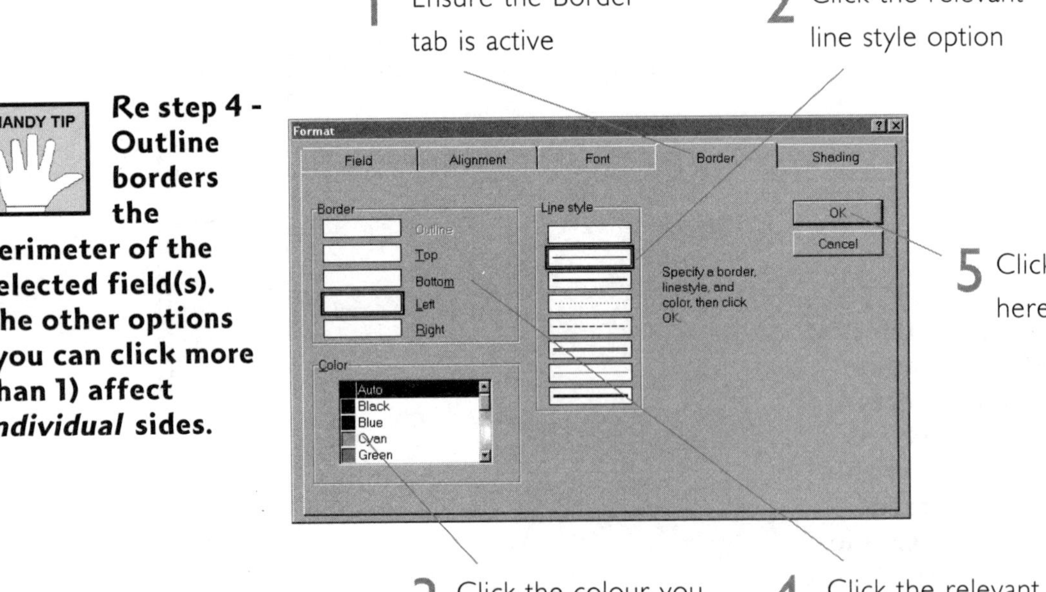

5 Click here

3 Click the colour you want to apply

4 Click the relevant border option(s) – see the tip.

Shading fields

In List view, you can apply the following to fields:

- a pattern

- a pattern colour

- a background colour

You can do any of these singly, or in combination. Interesting effects can be achieved by using pattern colours with coloured backgrounds.

Applying a pattern or background

First, select the heading(s) of the field(s) you want to shade. Pull down the Format menu and click Shading. Now carry out step 1 below. Follow steps 2, 3 or 4 as appropriate. Finally, carry out step 5:

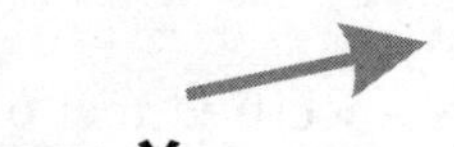

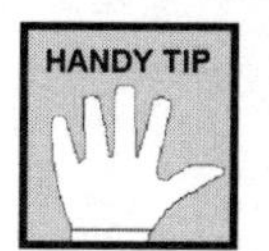

You can apply these in Form Design view, too. Note, however, that if no fields have been pre-selected they apply to the *whole* of the form.

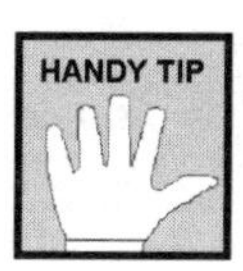

The Sample field previews how your background and pattern/colour will look.

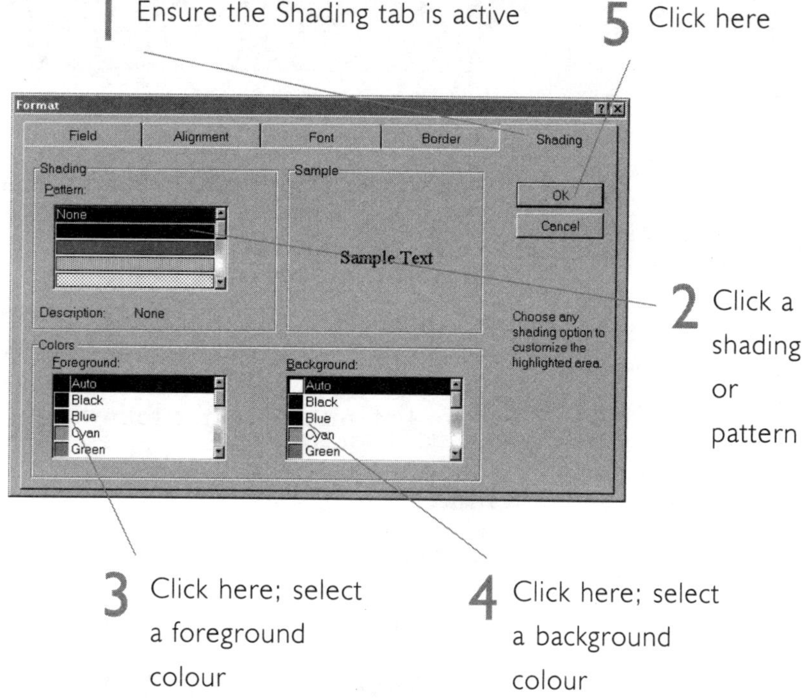

Find operations

The Database module lets you search for text and/or numbers. There are two basic options. You can:

- have the first matching record display

- view all records which contain the specified text or numbers

Searching for data

Pull down the Edit menu and click Find (or press Ctrl+F). Now carry out step 1 below, then *either* step 2 or 3. Finally, carry out step 4.

Type in the data you want to find

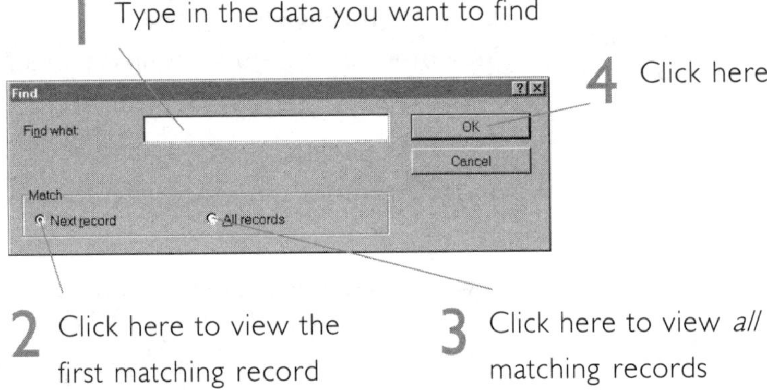

4 Click here

2 Click here to view the first matching record

3 Click here to view *all* matching records

Showing all records again

If you followed step 3 above, Works will only display matching records (other records in your database are inaccessible). To show all records again, pull down the Record menu and do the following:

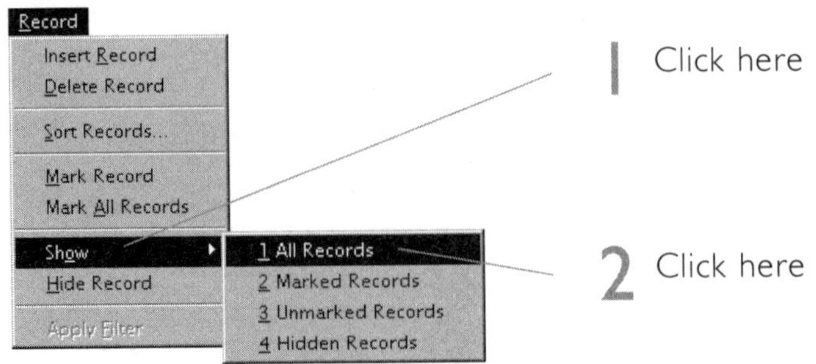

Click here

2 Click here

Search-and-replace operations

When you search for data, you can also – if you want – have Works replace it with something else.

You can specify the search direction:

You can only carry out a search-and-replace operation in List view.

Records	the search is left-to-right
Fields	the search is top-to-bottom

Running a search-and-replace operation

Pull down the Edit menu and click Replace. Now carry out step 1 below, then any of steps 2-3. Now do *one* of the following:

- Follow step 4. When Works locates the first search target, carry out step 5 to have it replaced. Repeat this process as often as necessary.

- Carry out step 6 to have Works find every target and replace it automatically.

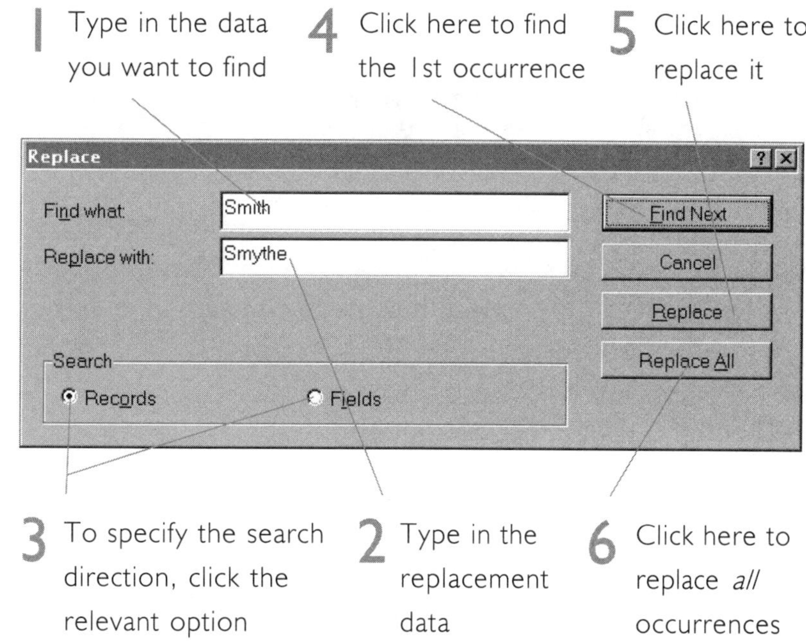

Page setup - an overview

When you come to print out your database, it's important to ensure the page setup is correct. Luckily, Works makes this easy.

Page setup features you can customise (in List view) include:

There are additional page setup options from within Form view - see the 'Other page setup options' topic later.

- the paper size

- the page orientation

- the starting page number

- margins

- whether gridlines are printed

- whether record and field headings are printed

Field headings

		Surname	First Name	Address	Post Code	Phone No.
1		Smith	Eugene	56 High St., Hunton		
2		Jones	Arthur	16 Trumping Camford		
3		Brown	Inigo	12 Codwalleder Ave. Slipforth		
4		Smith				

Record headings

Margin settings you can amend are:

- top

- bottom

- left

- right

When you save your active database, all page setup settings are saved with it.

Setting size/orientation options

The Database module comes with 11 pre-defined paper types which you can apply to your databases, in either portrait (top-to-bottom) or landscape (sideways on) orientation.

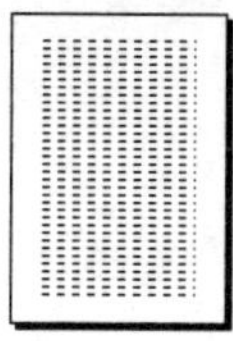

Portrait orientation

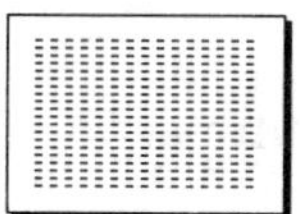

Landscape orientation

If none of the supplied page definitions is suitable, you can create your own.

Applying a new page size/orientation

Pull down the File menu and click Page Setup. Now carry out step 1 below, followed by steps 2-3 as appropriate. Finally, carry out step 4:

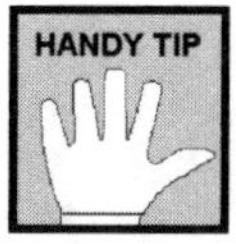

To create your own paper size, click Custom Size in step 3. Then type in width and height measurements in the Width & Height fields. Finally, carry out step 4.

1 Ensure this tab is active

2 Click an orientation

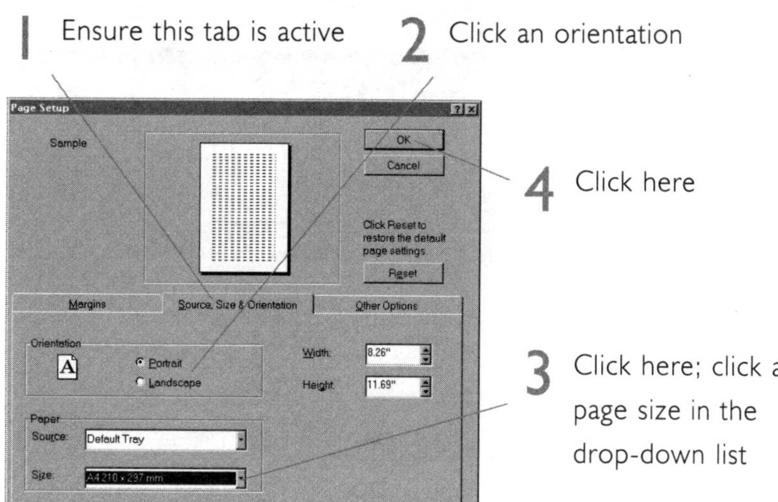

4 Click here

3 Click here; click a page size in the drop-down list

Setting margin options

The Database module lets you set a variety of margin settings. The illustration below shows the main ones:

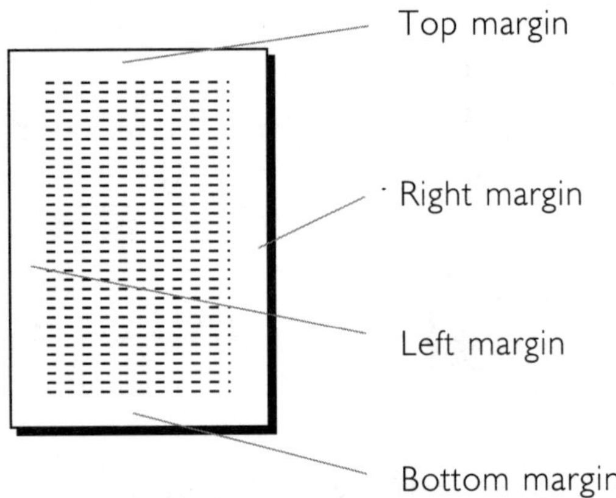

Applying new margins

Pull down the File menu and click Page Setup. Now carry out steps 1-3:

Ensure the Margins tab is active

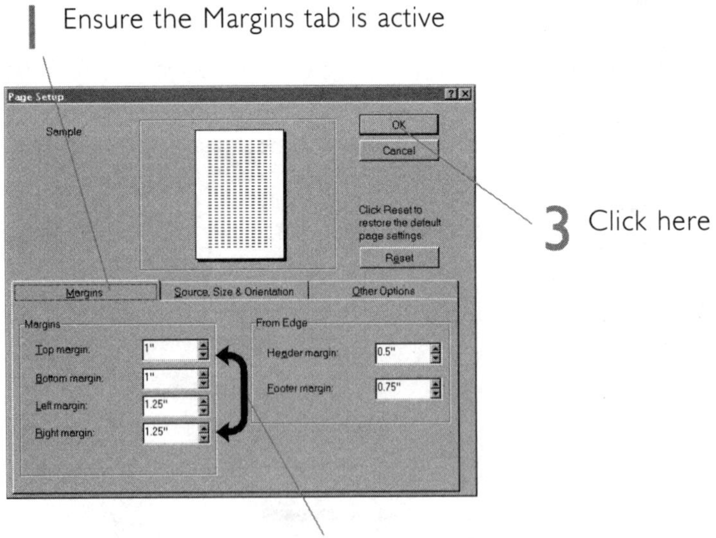

Other page setup options

You can determine whether gridlines and record/field headers print. These are demonstrated below:

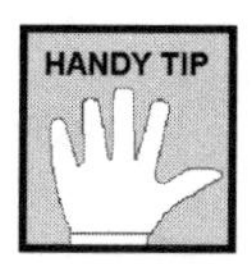

You can also set the page number for the first page in your database here (by default, '1') - see below.

Magnified view of field heading

Gridlines

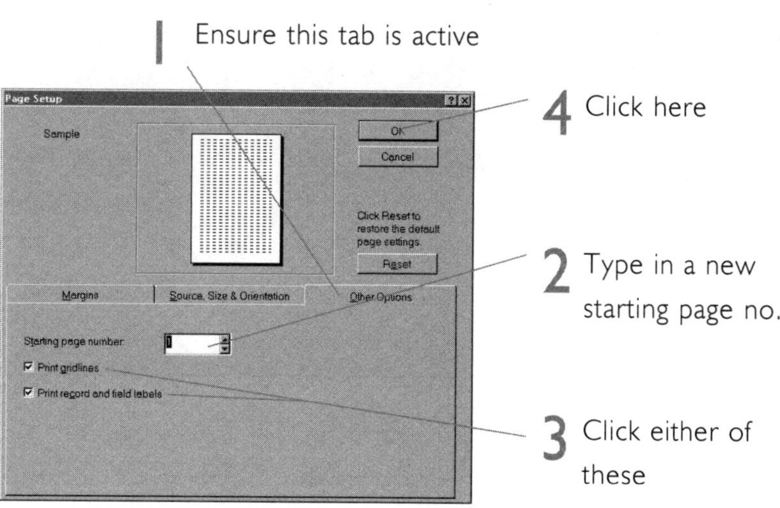

Record headings

Printing gridlines and record/field headings

Pull down the File menu and click Page Setup. Now carry out step 1 below, followed by steps 2-3 as appropriate. Finally, carry out step 4:

If you launch this dialog from within Form view, step 3 initiates lines between fields and/ or page breaks between records. You can also set the inter-record gap.

Ensure this tab is active

4 Click here

2 Type in a new starting page no.

3 Click either of these

Printing database data

When you print your data within List view, you can specify:

- the number of copies you want printed

- whether you want the copies 'collated'. This is the process whereby Works prints one full copy at a time. For instance, if you're printing four copies of a 20-page database, Works prints pages 1-20 of the first copy, followed by pages 1-20 of the second and pages 1-20 of the third... And so on.

- which pages you want printed

- the printer you want to use (if you have more than one installed on your system)

You can 'mix and match' these, as appropriate.

Starting a print run

Open the database which contains the data you want to print. Then pull down the File menu and click Print. Do any of steps 1-4. Then carry out step 5 to begin printing:

If you're printing from within Form view, you have a further choice. Click Current record only to limit the print run to the active record.

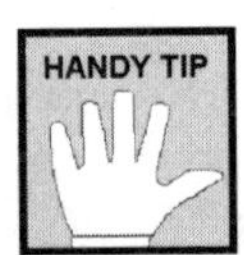

If you need to adjust your printer's internal settings before you initiate printing, click Properties. Then refer to your printer's manual.

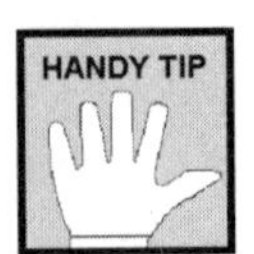

Click Draft quality printing to have your database print with minimal formatting.

Click here; select a printer from the list

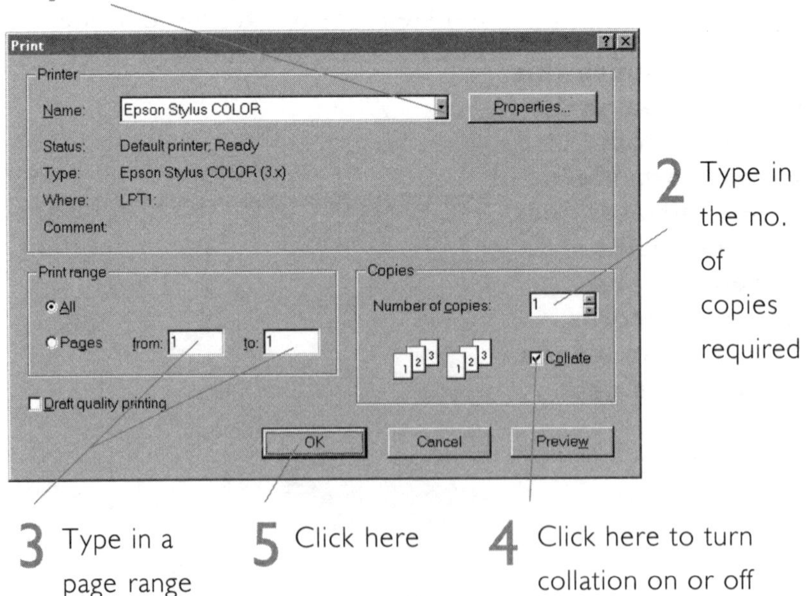

2 Type in the no. of copies required

3 Type in a page range

5 Click here

4 Click here to turn collation on or off

Index

Z